brilliant

online
marketing

How to use the Internet to market your business

Alex Blyth

Prentice Hall
is an imprint of

Harlow, England • London • New York • Boston • San Francisco • Toronto • Sydney • Singapore • Hong Kong
Tokyo • Seoul • Taipei • New Delhi • Cape Town • Madrid • Mexico City • Amsterdam • Munich • Paris • Milan

PEARSON EDUCATION LIMITED

Edinburgh Gate
Harlow CM20 2JE
Tel: +44 (0)1279 623623
Fax: +44 (0)1279 431059
Website: www.pearsoned.co.uk

First published in Great Britain in 2011

Pearson Education is not responsible for the content of third party internet sites.

ISBN: 978-0-273-73745-2

British Library Cataloguing-in-Publication Data
A catalogue record for this book is available from the British Library

Library of Congress Cataloging-in-Publication Data
Blyth, Alex.
  Brilliant online marketing : how to use the internet to market your business
     / Alex Blyth.
        p. cm.
  Includes index.
  ISBN 978-0-273-73745-2 (pbk.)
  1. Internet marketing. 2. Electronic commerce. 3. Marketing--Technological
innovations. I. Title.
  HF5415.1265B59 2010
  658.8'72--dc22

                                        2010039888

10 9 8 7 6 5 4 3 2 1
14 13 12 11 10

Typeset in 10pt Plantin by 30
Printed in Great Britain by Henry Ling Ltd., at the Dorest Press, Dorchester, Dorset

To Dad, who first inspired my love of words – and bought me my first computer

Contents

About the author

Alex Blyth is a freelance journalist, writer and training consultant. Born in 1974, he has a degree in Politics and Philosophy from the University of York.

Alex has written extensively on the topic of online marketing for publications such as *New Media Age*, *Revolution*, *B2B Marketing* and *Media Week*. Over the past decade, he has also put this specialist knowledge of online marketing into a broader business context, writing thousands of articles on topics as diverse as finance, recruitment, people management, training, employee benefits, direct marketing and public relations, for titles such as *The Independent*, *Accountancy*, *First Voice*, *Personnel Today*, *PR Week*, *Retail Week* and *Third Sector*.

His first book, *How to Grow Your Business for Entrepreneurs*, was published by Pearson in July 2009 and was quickly followed by *365 Ways to Cut Costs*, published by the Directory of Social Change in September 2009.

Alex is also building a successful media training business using many of the techniques he describes in this book.

Introduction

At the time of writing there were nearly 2 billion Internet users world-wide. It is the largest marketplace in history. For this reason, if no other, marketers have become very, very excited about the Internet. Marketers were there, excitedly watching the first fledgling company websites go live at the end of the last century. They were there enthusiastically exploring the potential of e-mail marketing, online advertising and search marketing.

No marketer worth his or her salt would ignore a channel that was as far-reaching as the Internet, that penetrated as deeply into our everyday lives, that was as affordable, trackable and malleable as the Internet.

It is for this reason that more and more businesses are using online marketing. Whether it is display advertising, e-mail marketing, social media engagement or some other form of online marketing, one thing is certain: online marketing is no longer a sideshow for technical enthusiasts. It is not even simply a useful supplement to traditional marketing. It is fast becoming *the* primary method by which businesses market their products and services. While economies, businesses and marketing budgets shrink, online marketing continues to grow.

However, enthusiasm and investment do not always translate into success. Indeed, online marketing presents marketers with as many questions as answers:

- How do you decide what to do – which form of online marketing is right for you?
- How do you tell a fad from a genuine opportunity?
- How do you know whether to lead or follow along the technology curve?

- How do you set realistic objectives?
- How do you retain the focus on marketing, not on technology?
- How do you know what you can do yourself?
- How do you pick the best suppliers at the right price and maintain a successful relationship with them?

Most of all, how do you pick out what really matters from all the hype, all the jargon and all the empty promises?

Corporate executives, entrepreneurs and students entering the business world all know that they need to get to grips with these questions. Failure to do so will limit the growth of their businesses and careers.

Yet online marketing is a difficult subject. Originally the preserve of technical enthusiasts, it has for too long been shrouded in mystery and technical jargon. Furthermore, it changes almost daily: in 1995 no one had heard of e-mail; in 2000 no one had heard of affiliate marketing; and in 2005 no one had heard of social media. Online marketing is a large and nebulous concept that is hard to pin down and understand. To cap it all, in many respects online marketing is completely different to offline marketing: many marketers struggle to adopt the mindset necessary to succeed in this new and radically different area.

This book answers all those questions, covering every aspect of online marketing, from website design through to cutting-edge techniques in online lead generation. The Internet is a global marketplace, and so while the focus of this book is on the UK, it makes use of some examples from other countries, such as the US.

This is not a history book, so you will not find detailed accounts of the birth of the Internet, its rise to prominence, and the many trials and tribulations marketers have had in making it work. There are many other books you can buy if you're interested in all that. This book is designed for the busy marketer who wants to find out as quickly as possible how they can make the Internet work for them. The focus is on understanding why you should do something and then on how you do it with as little trouble and cost as possible.

Each chapter deals with a different aspect of online marketing, from website design through to mobile marketing. In each you will find the following:

- a brief outline of what it is and advice on how you can decide whether or not it's a suitable marketing technique for your business;
- a clear step-by-step guide to doing it successfully;
- examples of companies that have done it successfully: some are small businesses with no more than a handful of employees, others are international brands, such as Marmite, Orange and Birds Eye;
- in-depth interviews with some of the UK's leading experts on the topic, in which they offer invaluable tips and tricks on how to succeed in this form of online marketing, as well as insight into what is cutting edge and new in this area.

The book has been written so that you can dip into any chapter and straightaway gather information and advice that is immediately useful. The aim is to make the seemingly complex world of online marketing more accessible to marketers, whatever their background, and to inspire action – in short, to give you everything you need to know to produce brilliant online marketing.

Acknowledgements

Online marketing is a fast-changing subject. With every day that passes someone comes up with a new technology, a fresh idea for new technology, or an original approach to using existing technology. All of it can help marketers reach their audiences more successfully. All of it matters.

For this reason no one person can ever hope to be the sole authority on the subject. No matter how deeply they immerse themselves in the world of online marketing, there will always be a brilliant new idea they miss. The idea of this book is to give you as many brilliant ideas as possible to help you market your products and services more effectively. So in researching this book I spoke to as many online marketing experts as I could find. I spoke to leading authorities on everything from website design, search marketing, online advertising, all the way through to mobile marketing and the emerging ideas on how to bring it all together as pull marketing.

I have included many of these interviews directly in the book. However, there were many other people who were invaluable sources of information, ideas and inspiration – Max Childs, EMEA Marketing Manager at Adobe Scene7, who had much of value to say on the use of rich media; Andy Budd, MD and founder of Clearleft, who gave me invaluable advice on the subject of user testing; and Paul Banham, Digital Creative Director at JWT, who gave me some very useful pointers on how to get the creative right in online advertising.

I would like to thank them and all the interviewees you see in the following pages, as well as all the hundreds of online marketing experts I have met, interviewed and written about over the past decade. I hope that I have been able to do justice to their cumulative expertise and produce a book which genuinely does give you, the reader, some brilliant ideas on how online marketing can work for you.

CHAPTER 1

Ten online marketing mistakes to avoid

'Human beings, who are almost unique in having the ability to learn from the experience of others, are also remarkable for their apparent disinclination to do so.'

Douglas Adams

What we'll cover in this chapter

Before we begin to look at what you *should* do with online marketing, we're going to look briefly at what you should *not* do. In this chapter you will find ten mistakes that people make all too frequently with online marketing.

Online marketing is a relatively new area and for many people it is an intimidating one. There is a great deal to learn, many new concepts to grasp and a vast morass of jargon to cut through.

As is always the case with a new area, there is no shortage of incautious enthusiasts ready to rush in, believing either that they don't need to learn the rules, that the rules don't apply to them, or that there's so much gold in the hills that a few failed mines will make little difference in the long run.

The result is that many people have lost a lot of money, damaged their reputations or just had their fingers burned. Don't make their mistakes. Before diving straight into the detail of this book, the nitty-gritty of website strategy, e-mail marketing and so on, take a look at these ten common errors – and then resolve never to make them yourself. Believe me – it will save you a lot of time, money and heartache.

Ten mistakes in online marketing

1 Believing it's all hype

There is a lot of hype about online marketing. Partly it is driven by the technological nature of the medium. Each year brings a new innovation, a new technique that you can use. First it was a website, then e-mail marketing, then online advertising and search, then more recently blogging and social media, and now all the talk is about mobile. There is always something new to get excited about.

It should be noted, though, that it is also driven by consultants and experts, many of whom have a vested interest in exaggerating the potential of online marketing. In fact, there are many charlatans who will enthuse about just how much money can be made from online marketing, but if you scratch a little beneath the surface you will discover that the only people who are making any real money from their work is themselves.

But just because there is an enormous amount of hype out there, do not fall into the trap of believing that it is nothing more than hype. Just because there are many charlatans out there, do not fall into the trap of believing that every so-called online marketing expert is a charlatan. That is unthinking cynicism and it will lead to you missing out on a great opportunity.

It is possible to use the Internet as a marketing channel to very good effect, and in this book there are many examples of companies that have done exactly that. They prove that, approached correctly, online marketing can help you generate leads, increase sales and boost profits.

2 Getting carried away

Equally, do not believe all the hype. Online marketing is no silver bullet, and it will not magically transform the marketing performance of your brand or your company. Too many people have taken the hype at face value, have rushed in, spending fortunes on the wrong things, and consequently have become disillusioned.

It is important to begin with a well-considered strategy and a small pilot scheme. Once you have refined your strategy so that you have a model that is generating new customers or sales leads, then – and only then – should you start to ramp up your investment of time and money.

Note that I refer to an investment of time as much as of money. One of the many benefits of online marketing is that it is increasingly mobile. You can access your campaigns and your work wherever you have a laptop and a broadband signal, or wherever you have your smartphone. You don't need to be in the office to be working on online marketing – you can do it during your daily commute, or even while you watch television in the evening.

While this is undoubtedly a benefit of online marketing, it can also be dangerous. Online marketing can be incredibly time-consuming and it can become addictive. There is so much you can do to track results, refine messages, tinker with imagery, grow your connections and so on. If you're not careful you can spend hours, days, weeks, even months of your time and achieve very little for it. This is especially true of social media. So keep a careful eye on how much time as well as how much money you spend on this.

> online marketing can be incredibly time-consuming

Finally, while we're on the subject of keeping a careful eye on things, look out for those charlatans. Treat all online marketing experts with a healthy scepticism. Question them closely on the business benefits they will produce. Do not confuse marketing metrics with business benefits. It does not matter how many people read your e-mails or how many Twitter followers you have. What matters is how many sales leads you generate, the uplift in sales the activity produces, or ultimately the rise in profits.

And never, ever let yourself be blinded by science. If an expert says something you don't understand, ask them to explain it more clearly. If you still don't understand it, tell them that you're not an online expert but you do understand business and marketing, so you need these new concepts explained in those traditional terms. If they still fail to explain themselves clearly, then thank them politely for their time and show them the door.

3 Failing to integrate the different types of online marketing

This book breaks up online marketing into its different elements of website design, search, e-mail marketing and so on, simply because that's the most logical way to tackle it, but in reality online marketing is most effective when the different elements are integrated, when they are carried out in combination with each other.

So, in your e-mail marketing you should draw attention to your blog and on your blog you should encourage people to sign up to receive your e-mail newsletter; your social media content should be designed to enhance your search performance; your online advertising should have the same look and feel as your website and drive traffic to your website; and so on.

In fact, you should never begin a campaign by saying 'Right, now I'd like to do some online advertising', or 'Our website hasn't been refreshed for some time – it's time we spent some money on it', or 'I've heard blogging is popular – let's start a blog'. Always begin by thinking about the business objectives that you want to achieve and then decide which online marketing techniques are most likely to help you achieve those objectives.

If you want to attract more visitors to your site, for instance, you should look into advertising and e-mail marketing; if you have plenty of visitors but not enough of them are turning into customers or leads, you might want to review your site; if you have a complex marketing message you want to convey to your audience, then a blog can be a good solution; and so on.

Far too many marketers begin to market online because they believe that all their competitors are doing it and so they could get left behind. This is perhaps one of the worst reasons for marketing online. Indeed, each chapter of this book begins with an explanation of why you should be interested in that subject and none of the reasons is 'because everyone else is doing this'. That is never a reason to spend your company's money on a marketing initiative. (If you don't believe me, go and ask your finance director!) Always begin with a clear understanding of how it will produce business benefits.

4 Failing to integrate online with offline marketing

In the same way, online marketing should never be a channel operating independently of your other marketing efforts; it should be a fully integrated part of your broader marketing strategy. So, you should promote your website and blog in your direct marketing, advertising, etc.

You should ensure that there is consistency of message, tone and creative across all your channels. Thus a potential customer could click on an online ad to receive a product sample through the post and would know when the sample arrived that it was from your company because the packaging was branded in line with the online ad.

5 Seeing it as free marketing

Online marketing can be cheap. In fact, other than your fixed IT costs, it can be free. Once you have e-mail for operational uses, it costs nothing to start e-mailing your prospects for marketing purposes. It costs nothing to start blogging, using social networking sites such as LinkedIn or Twitter. Online advertising generally costs a fraction of its offline equivalent.

However, do not fall into the trap of believing that online marketing costs nothing. Where it is free it requires an investment of time, for example producing high-quality marketing e-mails, writing blog content or building an online network of contacts.

Where it is inexpensive it usually requires you to invest in some other area. For example, online advertising space may be relatively low cost, but it becomes expensive if no one who clicks on your ads and visits your sites buys anything simply because you have built your site on the cheap.

If you want online marketing to be successful for you, you need to be prepared to invest time and money. It can certainly be cost-effective, but it is not cheap.

6 Delegating to the IT department

Online marketing may take place on computers and look like an IT job, but without doubt it is a job for marketers. In the early days of online marketing many companies saw it as an IT task and the result was websites that looked like pages of computer code, broken up only by gimmicky features that were there simply because the programmer had learned the code.

Perhaps the worst of all of these gimmicky features were the Flash-based animations. In the early days of website design software developer Adobe brought out Flash, a package that allowed users to produce short animations. Suddenly everyone was Walt Disney and it became impossible to open a website without first being subjected to a short animated film. It was incredibly annoying for users, who soon left these sites, and for marketers, who wanted to keep those users on their sites. The software – through no fault of its own, it should be noted – soon became a synonym for unnecessary online features. The focus now is on simplicity and on allowing users to get what they want from a site as quickly and as easily as possible.

This is not intended in any way to denigrate those who work in the IT department. If you are to make a success of your online marketing you will need a top-quality IT department that understands how to put your plans into action, that works with you to continually enhance campaigns and is there to advise you on what is technologically possible.

Bear in mind that this does not need to be an expensive department with dozens of highly paid experts – it can be a director who knows about IT. The point is that, while you need someone who can turn your vision into reality,

it needs to be you, the marketer, who has the vision

it needs to be you, the marketer, who has the vision.

The simple rule is that just because something is possible does not mean it should be done. Every aspect of your online marketing should conform to the fundamentals of marketing: you should identify your target audience, understand their specific needs and then develop campaigns that convince them your product or service will meet those needs.

7 Failing to get the right balance on user data

One of the major strengths of online marketing is that it presents you with an opportunity to gather a remarkable quantity of data on your customers and visitors and then use that data to improve future campaigns. It is therefore incredible how many companies fail to take advantage of this opportunity.

With every single campaign you run, ensure you build in some element of data capture. Integrate this with what you already know about your customers, be that on a sophisticated customer relationship management system or a simple spreadsheet. Then use this data to segment your campaigns more accurately, target them more precisely and improve their performance.

However, make sure you don't put your visitors through a grilling every time they arrive at your website. We have all experienced those websites: the ones you visit hoping to find some simple information but which insist you fill out a form with all your personal details. You probably also know how you tend to react. Unless that site has some highly valuable unique information, you just go elsewhere. Make sure you avoid becoming that site.

8 Trying too hard to go viral

According to research company Nielsen Online, at the end of 2009 there were just over 1.8 billion Internet users in the world. That was 26.6 per cent of the world's population and represented a 400 per cent increase from the start of that decade. That's a lot of people.

So, the Internet allows almost instant contact between billions of people on different continents right across the world. This means that if you can create a story, an image, a video or something else that people want to share with their friends, it can spread with the reach and speed of a virus. This is a particularly beneficial virus as it can send your sales into the stratosphere.

Perhaps the most obvious example of the power of viral marketing is Hotmail. Much of its early traction in the emerging e-mail hosting market was due to the simple fact that every time someone sent an e-mail from a Hotmail account, it automatically included an invitation to the recipient to set up a Hotmail account.

Another example was the Dove Evolution video. This showed an ordinary young woman – pretty, but not exceptionally so – sitting down and looking into a mirror. Over a time-lapse sequence we saw the make-up applied, the hair styled and the work done using picture-editing software until the end result: a billboard showing the girl transformed into a stunningly beautiful model. The film closed on the line 'No wonder our perception of beauty is distorted'. It generated such a buzz that according to some sources it was viewed more than 12 million times in the year after its 2006 release.

It would be great if you could emulate that success. However, you should avoid the trap of focusing only on the possibility of viral marketing. To talk to some online marketing experts you would think that unless a campaign goes viral it is a failure. Not only does this raise false expectations – very, very few campaigns create anything like the buzz of Hotmail or the Dove campaign – it also leads to campaigns that try too hard to achieve this effect.

In the worst cases these look inauthentic and damage a company's reputation. In the best cases they merely miss the greater potential of online marketing, which is to achieve genuine results by the steady, consistent application of marketing principles to this new channel.

9 Still expecting to control the conversation

In the days before the Internet revolution media space was scarce and so marketers who could afford to buy it could control what people read and, to a large extent, how their companies were perceived. Marketing was a considerably simpler affair than it is now.

One of the many society-changing effects of the Internet is that it has created an enormous space where people can go and say exactly what they want about companies. It is increasingly in this space that people's perceptions of brands are shaped. Think about the last significant purchase you made: did you look at a price-comparison site or a user-review site? The brand conveyed to you by the company's marketers probably had an effect on your ultimate decision – we still take note of offline marketing – but increasingly you and other consumers are relying on the messages we ourselves create online.

The repercussions of this for the marketing profession are seismic. No longer can marketers expect to dictate the conversation in the way they used to. Those who try tend to get fairly short shrift. The simple fact is that in this new form of marketing you cannot hope to control the conversation. It is a remarkably difficult fact for marketers to take on board. After all, just a decade ago that was more or less the description of a marketing role: marketers were paid to control how people saw the company. Now, though, it is all but impossible to do that. Instead, marketers need to learn how to influence online conversations. They need to learn how to use the tools so that they can listen to what people are saying about their brand. They need to take on board those comments and act accordingly, and then they need to use those online tools to let people know they have acted.

Let's not get carried away. Brands are still spending billions on television advertising, on direct mail and on public relations campaigns, and they are doing so because it works, because people are still susceptible to those traditional forms of marketing. However, many of them are also becoming adept at online engagement and influence. If you want to keep up with them, you need to learn these skills, too.

10 Laurel resting

Online marketing changes every day. Every time you arrive at work there is a new tool or a new channel or a new idea that could be useful to you. While you cannot hope to remain on top of all of them, you should be careful never to rest on your laurels.

You have never 'cracked' online marketing. You need always to be alert to what is out there. You must always be looking to refine your activities to take advantage of the very latest developments. It is a time-consuming and never-ending task, but get it right and it will be worth it.

 recap

Save yourself time, money and heartache by doing these five things and avoiding some of the most common errors people make with online marketing:

1 Be neither a wide-eyed enthusiast nor a close-minded cynic; rationally assess the potential of online marketing for your business and act accordingly.

2 Bring together the different parts of online and offline marketing to create a coherent and powerful strategy.

3 Be prepared to invest both time and money in online marketing.

4 Take a long-term view. Online marketing is too often seen as a quick fix, with sudden, dramatic results, but in fact you are more likely to succeed by understanding your audience, engaging in a two-way conversation with them and delivering what they want over a sustained period.

5 As the world of online marketing evolves continually, so you must remain open to new ideas and, where suitable, build them into your strategy.

CHAPTER 2

Your website – your conversion engine

'Good design keeps the user happy,
the manufacturer in the black and
the aesthete unoffended.'

Raymond Loewy

What we'll cover in this chapter

A company website is the foundation of almost every online marketing programme. In this chapter you will find:

- 15 steps to producing a website that converts visitors into customers;
- the story of how holiday company Cosmos improved its website and within a year increased online sales by 250 per cent;
- advice on website design and development from Keith Scarratt, who has spent the past two decades producing websites for the likes of Dairy Crest, Heathrow Express, GE and Anglo American.

Not so long ago websites were optional for businesses. It seems hard to imagine, but even as late as the end of the 1990s many businesspeople still thought websites were a little like computer games, something teenagers had fun with in their bedrooms, certainly not a serious marketing investment. As we have seen in the few years since, they quickly revised that opinion. Now it is hard to find a business that has no website. However, while the business world has been quick to see the potential of this new marketing channel, it has been slower to use it well.

Most businesses have now moved beyond simple brochure sites, involving acres of dense text and a lot of scrolling down. Legislation has encouraged them to make their sites easier to read, and complaints from customers have persuaded the majority to give up on complex Flash-based sites that took far too long to load. Most have even got to the point of including a phone number on every page, a feature that a remarkable number failed to include on early corporate sites.

However, for too many companies that is about as far as they have got. It's as though they got to 2005 and stopped trying. Maybe they were distracted by all the new, more exciting forms of online marketing – search, social media, affiliate marketing and so on. Maybe with the onset of the recession they had other priorities. Maybe they stopped getting complaints and so figured everything was fine. Whatever the reason, a great many companies have not taken their websites as far as they can and they are missing opportunities as a result.

Why is it so important to get your website right? Well, for one thing it may be your shopfront. Conversion rates from visitors to buyers hover around the 5 per cent mark for websites. If you were the manager of a shop that converted only 5 per cent of visitors into buyers, you would be worried. Conversion rates for bricks-and-mortar shops are usually above 90 per cent. You would certainly want to look into what was going wrong, why people were walking out without buying anything.

In the online world, most businesses tend to react by spending more on promoting their site, on attracting more people through the 'door'. This approach may make some commercial sense when it is cheaper to drive traffic than it is to fix the underlying problems, but people are becoming immune to online marketing methods and so it is proving ever more expensive to attract them to your site. In most cases, therefore, it makes much more sense to smarten up your shop, to make your website as effective as possible.

Even if you don't actively sell online, you need to consider the role a company website plays in researching a purchase. A poll conducted online by research firm Harris Interactive within the United States found that of 2,355 adults, 36 per cent use a website to gather information about a product, service or company before buying. It was by some margin the most important method of researching before making a purchase, way above face-to-face sales, print media advertising, review sites, a phone call to the company, or even friend recommendations through a social networking site.

brilliant tip

Don't believe the research, or think it applies only to purchasing in the US? Well, think about the last few significant, non-habitual purchases you made, whether as a consumer or a business buyer. How many times did you look at the company's website before committing? You may not even remember all the occasions you visited it. We have become so accustomed to checking a company's website that it has almost become an instinctive reflex. It may take no more than a glance to check it has a site that looks credible, or it may involve several hours of careful research. Either way, the lesson is clear: there is little point in you investing time and money in promoting your products, services or company if you have not first invested time and money getting your website up to scratch.

So, what are the steps you as a marketer should take to improve your website? It depends how much you have done already and how demanding your customers are. However, most marketers will find at least one area in the following 15 steps where they can improve their website.

15 steps to a brilliant website

1 Define objectives

Too few websites are properly planned. Businesses decide they need a site because their competitors have one, because everyone else is getting one, or because they want to be seen as forward-thinking pioneers in the digital age. All too rarely do the marketers at the business spend time carefully thinking about why they need one and what they want to achieve with it. The result tends to be websites that fail both to give visitors what they want and to provide the business with the results it wants.

too few websites are properly planned

You should always begin by devising a strategy for your website. Regardless of whether you are building a site from scratch or you are revamping an existing site, or whether your site is a brochure site with just a few pages or an enormous e-commerce operation, you should begin by defining exactly what you want it to achieve.

As we've already seen, your site is there to convert the traffic your promotional activity drives there, but what do we mean by converting them? Do you want them to buy something on the site? Do you want them to pick up the phone and arrange an introductory meeting with you? Do you want them to sign up to attend an event or receive a white paper? Whatever conversion means for your business, if you begin with clarity on it you will have a much greater chance of producing a website that achieves those goals.

However, avoid the trap of making your site only about your company. You want it to achieve certain goals, but those goals involve other people doing something, so think about those other people. Who are they? Why do they visit your site? What do they want from it? Put yourself in their shoes. Or go a step further and ask them directly. Give them what they want and they will be more likely to give you what you want.

2 Design your site architecture

Once you are clear about what you want to achieve and what your visitors want from your site you will be able to devise your site architecture. From your homepage you will offer visitors several options and from this second level they will be able to drill down to a third and possibly a fourth. If visitors have to click down below a third level their attention will wander; by a fourth they will have left your site. It can take time to get this architecture just right, but it is time well spent – provide a logical structure that presents visitors with all the information they want and you are well on the way to producing an effective website.

3 Pick a domain name

The next step is to create the content for your site. This should begin with your domain name. If you already have a domain name which is well known by your target audience, unless it is a particularly bad name you will be best advised to stick with it. If you have a blank canvas then put some thought into your choice of name. Make sure it describes what your company does and is sufficiently memorable.

 **example**

The name game

Your choice of domain name matters, but don't get too hung up on it. Bear in mind that Google, Cingular and Joost were chosen only because googol.com, singular.com and juiced.com were already registered.

4 Draw up an initial list of keywords

We'll look at search in detail in the next chapter, but with website design it is never too early to think about search. Search engines rely on keywords and key phrases to identify websites and direct traffic to them. So before you begin to write any of your content, draw up a list of the words and phrases that are key to your business. Try to use them when you name your pages and in your copy. It will make the process of optimising your site much easier when you get to it.

5 Write your copy

Then it's time to dive in and write your copy. Many firms hire a professional copywriter to do this, but if you prefer to do it yourself, bear in mind the mantra 'less is more'. Good business writing is always simple and direct, and this is never more the case than with web copy. Use as few words as possible to make your point. Avoid large chunks of text – break them up with bullet points. Hook the reader in with compelling titles and opening sentences.

 'I am sorry I have had to write you such a long letter, but I did not have time to write you a short one.'

Blaise Pascal

6 Consider rich media

Bear in mind, however, that website content need not be purely words. Broadband is now so prevalent that more and more websites are able to make use of audio and video. This rich media is more engaging for visitors than simple text and allows you to bring products or people to life. It's all about presenting products in such a way that the consumer can inspect items from every angle, view fine details and compare colours, see how clothes hang and create outfits, see how electrical products operate or put furniture combinations together. Or they can see their future account manager describing how she works.

If you introduce any of these rich media elements, ensure that your visitors will be able to access them as quickly and easily as they would simple text. Make it complicated and they just won't use it. Get it right, though, and this can be a valuable tool in increasing the amount of time people spend on your site, the number of times they visit and the number who convert into customers. Indeed, many experts are predicting that the future of websites is to become more like television and radio and less like a book.

7 Allow users to generate content

Technology has advanced to a point where visitors can access rich media. It is also allowing those visitors to create their own content. This ranges from posting a comment on your site to filming and uploading a video. Think about how you could use this type of user-generated content on your site. Properly deployed, it can transform your site from somewhere people visit occasionally to find out about your company to somewhere they think of as part of their online home, as somewhere they care about.

8 Set up a content management system

Once you have produced your content – or put in place the systems to allow visitors to produce content for your site – you need to devise a way of managing it. Content that is not managed quickly dates or diminishes in quality. Ensure you have first an easy-to-use back-end system for updating your site, and second a group of people who do this regularly and competently.

9 Think about re-purposing your content

In later chapters we will look at how you can use blogs, social media and online PR to promote your site and your business. All of these activities require large amounts of high-quality content. So by developing website content that can be re-used as blog posts, white papers and so on, you will save yourself time in the future.

10 Convey your brand

Once you have your content, you need to move on to the look and feel of your site. While everyone can write to some degree and so writing your own copy is an option, very few of us can design sites or write the code to actually build them, so you will almost certainly need to hire professionals for this stage.

However, just as it helps to have a basic understanding of how a car works when you take yours for repairs, so it is important you understand the principles of good website design when briefing and working with your website designer. The first point to be aware of is that the site should reflect your brand. This means more than ensuring your logo is on the home page. Just as you want your shopfront, your office lobby or your receptionist's tone of voice to reflect what is different and special about your company, so should your website.

Your choice of designer and developer can have a huge bearing on the success of your website, so take great care in your selection. Always look at previous examples of their work to check they produce work that fits with your brand and your objectives. Ensure that an easy-to-use content management system is built in, so you're not reliant forever more on the designer and developer when you want to make updates. Agree a plan in advance for how the site will be optimised for search, how it will be secured and how it will be hosted. Don't accept payment by an hourly rate, as it is far better to agree a price upfront and eliminate the possibility of unpleasant surprises. Don't be afraid to demand changes to the initial design. Don't be bamboozled by jargon.

> agree a plan in advance for how the site will be optimised

Above all else, look for a designer and developer with whom you get on and who has a clear understanding of your business objectives.

11 Simplify, simplify, simplify

Designers like to design and site developers like to develop, which is all well and good until they get carried away and produce fussy designs and unnecessary site features simply because they can, not because those designs or features add to the site. Question at every stage how each feature of the site helps to achieve your strategic objectives. If something doesn't, then ditch it.

Aim for simplicity. Make information easy to find. Insist on a navigation system that is so easy and intuitive to use you barely notice it is there. Ensure visitors can always return to your homepage with a simple click, make sure links change colour when a visitor clicks on them, and finally, compare your site to similar sites. People appreciate design that is similar to what they already know, so make sure nothing on your site is so out of the ordinary that it will detract from what is unique and special about your message.

12 Make it accessible

Your site should be accessible to people of all abilities and disabilities. This is more than just the right thing to do, it also makes good business sense. With a few simple tweaks to your site you can greatly increase the number of people who are able to use it. For definitive advice on this, visit the website of the World Wide Web Consortium at www.w3.org.

13 Gather feedback from visitors

Before you launch your revamped site you should put it through some rigorous testing. This should begin with you and your colleagues using it, making sure every link works, all the copy is flawless and all is as it should be. Then you should ask your customers for their views.

Don't assume that you or your colleagues in marketing know what your customers want. When DIY chain Wickes was developing a new website, it showed five different designs of a proposed sign-in page to a sample of around 500 marketers. They were asked which one customers were likely to prefer. When the responses were compared with the results from live customer testing, it turned out only 4.6 per cent of the marketing experts had guessed right.

14 Begin user testing

Of course, what people actually do on your site might be very different to what they say they do. So as well as asking them what they think of your site, you can observe them using it. This should begin with Google Analytics, a free tool that is easy to use and will give you information on numbers of visitors, where they go on your site and so on.

It should then progress to cheap tools such as Silverback, which allow you to capture screen activity and video record users' reactions. You will be able to get a remarkable level of insight and improvement from just these tools. If you want to take it even further there are more expensive tools on the market that allow you to track eye movements on site, to psychologically profile your users to find out what motivates them, or to run a series of multivariant tests to assess the effect that even the smallest changes to the design will have on conversion rates.

Finally, an emerging area is neuro web design, where you can use biometric feedback to understand the effect certain design decisions are having. At the moment commercial bio-feedback is really limited to aspects such as heart rate and galvanic skin response. However, in the next few years we will see more devices that will be able to pinpoint the effects your websites are having on particular parts of the brain and then design around that.

15 Adapt and refine your site

Whatever you do, don't put in all this work only to then move on to a new project, forgetting about your website and allowing it to quietly moulder away, becoming less and less relevant. You must keep it fresh with new content and you must use the results of all this testing and visitor analysis to continually refine your site, giving visitors more of what they want and improving your conversion rate.

 **example**

Cosmos

Cosmos is the UK's largest independent tour operator. It is part of the Globus group of companies, a family-run organisation established in 1928, which also encompasses Cosmos Tourama, Avro, Monarch Airlines and Archers Direct.

With more than 40 years' experience, Cosmos is one of the most established names in the travel industry. It started out in the 1960s offering holidays to just a few Mediterranean destinations, but now takes more than half a million people to more than 35 destinations around the world each year.

In June 2006 the company decided it was time to revamp its website and called in digital agency Digital Marmalade. It set the agency the objectives of increasing the conversion rate from visitors to customers and increasing the revenue the website generated.

Digital Marmalade started with a scoping and feasibility study. This began with a full review of the existing site – the content, the technology deployed and the maintenance required. Next, the agency investigated what Cosmos's competitors were doing. Finally, it ran workshops with Cosmos's key staff and suppliers to hear their views on the site and get some insights into how it could be improved.

It soon became apparent that the site needed more than a simple redesign. The site was effectively a holiday search box, which when filled in brought back matching results, but there were three fundamental problems with the way it worked. First, visitors could book only around 50 per cent of the results returned. Second, many of the company's holiday products could not even be found on the website and were therefore unbookable through the web. Third, and equally important, there were no fixed pages. Search engines need content that is fixed so they can index it and match it to the search criteria. Content that changes, such as holiday offers, is less appealing to search engines and so this lack of fixed content meant that Cosmos had a poor search engine presence.

Digital Marmalade recommended to Cosmos that it should scrap the whole site and build it again from scratch. It stressed the importance of developing a coherent digital strategy which would shift the company's culture away from the traditional holiday sales channels, such as brochures and travel agencies. It was a radical proposal, but the senior management at Cosmos accepted it and gave Digital Marmalade their full backing.

Work began on the new site in the second half of 2006. The first step was to standardise the geographical classification on the site so that visitors could access any resort with just two clicks. This provided the structure for the site. The next step was to rewrite the site's content and source fresh images for all destinations, regions and resorts. Information was standardised across hotels and the company invested in high-quality images of hotels. All this content needed to be made available in a logical page structure, which would be easy for the search engines to access and read. Next came usability. Digital Marmalade redesigned the entire booking process, from search to buying extras such as excursions, car hire and travel insurance, all the way through to confirmation. The main objective was to ensure that the booking process was as straightforward as possible and that it allowed for easy up-sell opportunities.

Marcus Brennand, MD at Digital Marmalade, reports that although the website build was fairly straightforward, this project was not without its challenges. 'The major obstacles were actually cultural,' he says. 'The website build, although hard work and intense, went very smoothly, but the major issues were in changing the mindsets of the Cosmos commercial, marketing and media teams so they were web focused. Running a holiday website is very different to running a holiday business through brochures and travel agencies. Online, things change in real time and so people need to be manning the stations at all times. Prices and availability of product need to be monitored and adjusted all the time. ID data isn't exact, systems break or products aren't displayed properly. So, our greatest challenge was being an external agency trying to take people outside of their comfort zone and changing the way they do their jobs.'

Fortunately, the project had the backing and direct involvement of senior management. This was essential for getting it through the difficult early days, but once the site began to generate more revenue and all the other key metrics started to rise, everyone quickly came on board. Brennand says that for him the highlight of the project was seeing the Cosmos team actively embracing the website, enjoying their new roles and building on their web skills.

The figures have also been impressive. Within the first year of going live the website was regularly taking bookings of more than £1 million a week. That was a 250 per cent increase on the previous year. Conversion rates have increased massively and at the time of writing were above the travel industry's average.

Looking ahead, Digital Marmalade is working with Cosmos on an iPhone application for booking holidays, it has transferred all the Cosmos holidays into a Monarch Travel Portal and it is investigating the possibility of including reviews on the site and building a presence in the social media world.

Brennand concludes with this advice for others looking to replicate the success of this website project: 'Plan thoroughly. The more planning you can put in, the more successful the build will be. Include all key members of your team and important suppliers in this process. Don't be afraid to challenge everything. Finally, keep your nerve, trust your convictions and stick to the plan.'

Expert interview: Keith Scarratt, Director of Strategy & Planning, Flipside Group

The Flipside Group is a leading digital marketing agency with more than 50 people working out of its head office ten minutes from Guildford, Surrey. It has worked on some of the largest website design projects in the UK for clients such as Dairy Crest, Heathrow Express, GE and Anglo American.

Before joining Flipside as Director of Strategy & Planning, Keith Scarratt spent two decades working in brand and integrated marketing solutions. He started off at Saatchi & Saatchi, where he helped develop some of the world's leading brands, including Disney, Burger King, Pizza Hut, Pampers, Ariel and Visa International. He then moved on to a role as a strategic marketing consultant within Martin Sorrell's WPP Group of companies, where he developed the brands of Royal & Sun Alliance, British Telecom, Securicor and Barclays. Finally, he moved clientside as Group Marketing Director for the Imagine Group.

He is, then, someone well worth listening to on the subject of website design and development.

AB: Hi Keith. Could you begin by telling me about the Flipside Group?

KS: The Flipside Group was founded in the mid-1990s, back in the days when businesses needed persuading that they should have a website and that it could be a useful marketing tool. In the 15 years since then, not only has the world of website building changed out of all recognition, but Flipside has thrived and become involved in more and more exciting and interesting website design projects.

AB: What do you believe is the fundamental thing to get right with website design?

KS: It's absolutely vital to get your content right. It has to be unique and it has to engage your audience. Without that you're wasting your time.

AB: How would someone reading this book go about designing a website that has that sort of unique and engaging content?

KS: You've got to start by asking yourself what your objectives are. Too many companies rush into designing their sites, writing their copy and then promoting them, without spending time on the crucial planning stage. First of all, ask yourself why you want a website. What do you want it to achieve?

Is it to communicate your brand? Is it to convey leads to sales? Or both? Or something else altogether? Beginning with clarity on this will help you get the rest right.

AB: OK. Then what?

KS: You then need to build the wireframe. This is where you identify the main content areas of your site. What is it that people want to see and read? What is it you want to show them and tell them? Think about your priorities and use those to inform decisions on what should go in different areas. Remember at this stage that less can be more. Visitors are unlikely to want to spend a long time searching through your site, so ensure they can get what they want quickly.

AB: What about content? What's your advice on that?

KS: In my opinion, too many websites focus on what the company does, who they are and how they do it, to the detriment of the most important sales message: how they benefit their customers. People need to put themselves in the shoes of someone visiting the site and ask what information will most interest those visitors.

However, you can do more than just imagining what visitors will want to see or how they will react to certain content: you can ask them. Don't forget to talk to your customers and prospects. Get their feedback on your site. Ask what they like, what they don't like. Solicit their ideas for how it could be improved. You'll be amazed by what they come up with. On top of this everyone should use Google Analytics. It's free and surprisingly sophisticated. You'll get a long way with that product before you find you have to start paying for more in-depth analytics.

AB: What about user testing? Are you a fan?

KS: Very much so. You know how Google moved its paid-for results to the top left of the page from the righthand column? It was because their user testing showed them that people looked first at the top left of the screen. We use a product called Tobii Technology for our testing. It actually tracks eye movements on a site and so is pretty expensive. However, for as little as £3 a month, you can get tools showing heatmaps of where people click on your site.

AB: As we all know, the world of website design is continually evolving. What do you see as the next big thing on the horizon?

KS: The launch of the new version of HTML, HTML 5, will provide the impetus for the next generation of websites. It's going to make it much easier to embed video in websites and I think that's where we'll see the most important developments over the next couple of years. Websites will be less like books and more like television, with much of the content increasingly provided by users. You have only to look at the popularity of YouTube to see the potential in this area.

AB: So, how would you summarise your advice on how to build a successful website?

KS: Make sure you invest enough resources. I've seen too many companies fail to resource their website design and development properly, and so end up with sub-standard sites that either fail to exploit an opportunity or, in the worst cases, cause significant problems for the company. You can't just dip in and out. You need to keep your site properly maintained and constantly updated. Very often that involves a full-time resource.

Finally, make sure you join things up. Promote your website in all your offline communications and ensure that your website reflects your broader brand. It is already one of the most powerful expressions of that brand and in the years to come is likely to become even more important. You simply can't afford to get it wrong.

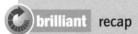 **recap**

1 Your website is your conversion engine. If it's not converting visitors to sales then all your other online marketing work is wasted.

2 Don't settle for a website that did the job back in 2005. The world of websites moves on rapidly, and while you don't need to incorporate every latest fad, you do need to ensure you are making the most of every available technology, service and idea.

3 Follow the 15 steps above to create your website and above all else ensure focus on the user. At the very least, make it straightforward for them to use. If possible, make it fun for them to use.

CHAPTER 3

Search engine optimisation

'Looking at the proliferation of personal web pages on the net, it looks like very soon everyone on earth will have 15 Megabytes of fame.'

M.G. Siriam

What we'll cover in this chapter

Search is the most important way of telling potential customers about your website, so in this chapter you will find:

- seven steps to moving your website up the search engine rankings;
- advice on search engine optimisation from Neil Jackson, who has been at the forefront of this industry as it has emerged over the past 12 years;
- the story of how vehicle leasing company Nationwide Vehicle Contracts implemented a search engine optimisation (SEO) programme which produced a 93 per cent increase in website visitors in the first year, and which allowed it to stop spending money on paid-for searches, resulting in a saving of £30,000.

A website that reflects your brand, excites visitors and converts prospects into customers is a vital tool in online marketing. It is, however, only the beginning of your journey. Your next step is to encourage people to visit that site. Because, unlike in the real world where you could build a shop which beautifully showcased all the products your customers want to buy and people would just wander in, on the Internet there is no such thing as passing trade. You have to actively promote your site – and that's what much of the rest of this book is about.

As we will see, there are many techniques for attracting visitors to your site. Search is the big one though. According to Jupiter Research, 80 per cent of Internet users find new websites through a search.

⤢ brilliant impact

According to Nielsen Online, in March 2010 in the UK 90 per cent of all Internet searches were conducted on Google, 5.78 per cent were on Yahoo, 2.98 per cent on Bing and 1.24 per cent on others.

In the US it is a little more even – Google gets 65 per cent, Yahoo 14 per cent, Bing 13 per cent and others 8 per cent. But the message is clear: at the moment, search means Google.

That fact is worth restating: 80 per cent of Internet users find new websites through a search. They don't hear about it from a friend or colleague. They don't see it on a poster or in a television ad. They don't even link to it from a social media site. They go to a search engine – almost certainly Google – and they input some words and they go to the sites that the search engine suggests.

That is a radical transformation in the way we research purchases. There was nothing remotely like it only a decade ago and yet search has insinuated itself deeply into how we live our lives. Think about how you made your latest significant purchase. I don't mean the last sandwich you bought; I mean something like the last MP3 player or car or accountant. Chances are you used a search engine at some point in the process.

In many ways this dominance of search is a good thing. In the late 1990s, in the run-up to the dotcom boom, before search really took off, if you wanted to attract visitors to a website you either had to be an established brand launching an online version (Tesco.com, dell.com) or you had to raise awareness the old way – by spending a small fortune advertising your business (lastminute.com, expedia.com). If you didn't have at least a seven-figure sum you weren't even in the game. Now, you don't need that much money at all – you just need to know how to optimise your site for the search engines and you need to spend a lot of time getting it right.

Seven steps to moving your website up the search engine rankings

Search engine optimisation – also known as natural or organic search – is a fairly straightforward process. That does not mean that it is cheap or easy. It requires a significant investment of time and that is one of the reasons why many people choose to bring in SEO experts to do it all for them. If you have more money than time, that is a perfectly good solution. They are specialists so will probably be able to do it much more rapidly and successfully than you anyway.

If, however, you simply feel that SEO is a mysterious and dark art, the secrets of which are known to only a chosen few, and so, even though you can't really afford it, you are going to spend money on an expert, that is a bad idea. Many of those experts tend to give the impression that SEO is not for the uninitiated or the faint-hearted. Don't believe them. It is genuinely straightforward. Dedicate a bit of time to following these seven steps and watch your website rise up the search engine rankings.

1 Read the search engine's own guidelines

If you needed further proof that SEO is not a secret art, you should be reassured by the fact that the main search engines all offer their own advice on how to optimise your website:

● www.google.com/webmasters

You should start by reading that advice and you should consult it regularly. Search is a relatively new area of marketing activity and the rules change slightly all the time. The search engines want you to have a site that is easy for the right people to find, so they are a good source of information on the very latest rules.

> search is a relatively new area of marketing activity

2 Hook up to good blogs on SEO

You won't find out everything from the search engines themselves, however. This book will give you more than you would discover there, but in order to keep on top of this constantly evolving area you should regularly read some of the good blogs on the subject. These will be enough to get you started:

- http://searchengineland.com/
- www.seroundtable.com/
- www.seomoz.org/blog
- http://searchenginewatch.com/
- www.nma.co.uk/channels/search/

3 Make your site easy to crawl

Search engines work by sending out 'spiders' to read the text on websites and then index them. A web spider is a program search engines send out to fetch web pages. They are called spiders simply because they crawl across the Web. They are also known as web crawlers, automatic indexers or bots.

You need to make it easy for spiders to access and navigate your site. This means giving them text. Basically, these spiders are unable to see Flash-based content, content generated through JavaScript, content displayed as images and much of the other rich media that make websites look appealing.

So you need to ensure you have a good balance between text and rich media. Too much of one will mean no one can find out about your site; too much of the other will mean people can find it and reach it, but once there they'll probably wish they hadn't.

4 Pick the right keywords

You also need to use the right words. Or, to be more accurate, you need to use the words that the people you want to attract are putting into search engines. In simple terms, if on your site you use the word 'tiger' a lot, you will appear high in the search engine rankings when people search for 'tiger'. This is great if you are marketing a product or service to do with tigers, not good if your business has nothing to do with tigers. It is important that the words on your site are closely related to what your business markets. The choice of these keywords and key phrases is therefore vital. Think about the words your customers might use to find you. Look at what results these produce. Use free tools such as Google AdWords that will help you decide the best words for your site.

It is likely that before long you will have dozens and dozens of possible keywords and phrases. You should choose just a handful to begin with, get that working and then move on to the rest. Pick a mix of general terms that will produce a large number of results and more specific terms that will produce fewer, better targeted results.

5 Work keywords into your copy and your page titles

The next step is to work these key words and phrases into the copy on your website. Pay particular attention to your page titles. Search engines give a lot of weight to title tags, so make good use of your key words and phrases in these.

One note of caution: don't over-optimise at the expense of copy that makes sense and is interesting to read. The search engines are increasingly wise to copy that is written purely for the sake of optimisation, and if a computer program can spot that a piece of text doesn't make much sense, visitors to your website will certainly do so. They won't stay long.

6 Encourage links to your website

After keywords and phrases, the most important element of SEO is links. Links are the lifeblood of the web. At the time of writing, around 70 per cent of Google's algorithm was link-based. That means it looks for the relevance and quality of those links. So you need to persuade owners of other websites to include links to your site. Those links will be even more powerful if the websites have a high search ranking. The search engines are effectively rating how useful your site is likely to be to their users, so if you have a well-regarded site linking to you it assumes you should be similarly well regarded.

By far the best way of doing this is providing high-quality content on your website. This could be news on a particular topic, or offers that excite consumers, or a white paper that people want to download. Whatever it is, if it is of real value to people then you will enjoy the coincidence of several factors: the search engine spiders will rate it highly, other websites will link to it and visitors will engage with it.

Content really is king online.

There are other ways of getting sites to link to yours. You can submit your site to the Open Directory Project (www.dmoz.com) for a free listing. You can arrange reciprocal links with well-regarded sites. And you can tell people about your site. Tell everyone you meet. Mention it when you post comments on other people's blogs, when you write your own blog, when you Tweet or update your LinkedIn status. We will come on to look in more detail about how you do this, but for now start getting into the habit of promoting specific links to your site.

> you can arrange reciprocal links with well-regarded sites

7 Continually refine

The final step is to keep refining your SEO activity. You need to remain abreast not only of trends in what your potential customers are searching for but also of how the very rules of the game are changing. For example, in 2009 Google launched its 'Web History' feature, which means it also factors in previous searches and clicks into what it decides to show you as a result of a search. No longer are search results based solely on on-page relevancy and third-party links pointing into a site, now a user's history is also a factor. It is a dramatic change and one that could significantly alter how marketers approach search.

You need to be on top of these developments and adapt your activity accordingly. One of the best things about SEO, however, is that although it takes a sizeable initial investment of effort, once you have your campaign up and running it requires only frequent, minor tweaks to ensure it continues to produce a steady stream of traffic to your site.

Neil Jackson, Director of Search, Tamar

Tamar describes itself as a search and social conversion agency. Essentially, this means it uses search engine optimisation and social media to generate sales for its customers. Neil Jackson, Director of Search, has been involved in search marketing for more than 12 years. Way back in the early days of the industry he was optimising websites on search engines such as Alta Vista, Lycos and Excite. Now he is Director of Search at Tamar, where he runs campaigns for major brands in the ultra-competitive online sectors of finance, retail and travel.

AB: You work in some tough, competitive sectors, right?

NJ: Absolutely. This really is the sharp end of natural search. But despite the intense competition, we regularly dominate over 50 per cent of the first page of Google for their clients' most competitive search terms.

AB: Impressive. It can't be cheap for your customers to achieve that.

NJ: No, results like that don't come cheaply. Too many people think that natural search is free. They're wrong. No matter what scale of operation you are running, you need to involve time and effort in terms of the site build, design, structure and content.

AB: Does that mean that it's more expensive than paying for sponsored links?

NJ: Not necessarily. Get a campaign right and you can drive high volumes of traffic at very low cost. We have many clients who have had such success with their SEO that they've been able to reduce or redirect the money they were spending on paid search.

AB: Sounds good. So, what's the secret?

NJ: Simply put, natural search is about creating websites which answer user 'questions' as relevantly as possible. The search engines all have one goal in mind and that is to be able to give users access to the information they require as quickly as they can. Help them do that and you'll shoot up the rankings.

AB: Yes, but how do we do that?

NJ: You must understand your sector or niche. For most sites a so-called white hat approach is recommended – that is, following the guidelines of the search engines. Playing it safe is the best way to start until you get a feel for what you need to do. If you push too hard you may incur penalties, which can vary from reduced rankings to complete removal from the Google index.

AB: So, in practical terms, what does that mean? How do I get started today?

NJ: Read the Google Webmaster guidelines. Visit forums where people are discussing SEO. Read, learn and understand before putting anything into practice. See what your online competitors are doing and understand why. You do not need to copy exactly what they do as this will not work, but you can build an overall picture of what it can take to be successful.

AB: That makes sense. Is there anything else you would recommend?

NJ: Research and knowledge are the keys to success. Know what your target audience is searching for and know how to give it to them. Be constantly ready to adapt to the ever-changing algorithms, whether at a technical or a content level. You also need to be patient and to constantly test.

AB: What's new, interesting and cutting edge in the world of SEO right now?

NJ: Real-time search and personalised search offer great opportunities for companies which are agile and are prepared to engage in an open way with their users. Trying to remain in 100 per cent control of your message will hold you back. Being open and sharing will gain you more than you will lose, as long as your approach is thought through.

AB: Finally, then, what one piece of advice would you offer someone who is looking to push their site up the natural search engine rankings?

NJ: Don't think you can't compete. Search engines are democratic – if you offer the right solution for your users and for the search engines, you will succeed.

 **example**

Nationwide Vehicle Contracts

Established in 2002, Nationwide Vehicle Contracts is a provider of car and van leasing for businesses and private individuals. It operates partnerships with the UK's largest vehicle-management banking groups, including Lex Vehicle Leasing, Lombard Vehicle Management and Network Vehicles, meaning it can offer good discounts as well as an appealing range of vehicles.

However, by 2005 David Johnson, the owner of the company, had decided that for a company that relies entirely on its website for sales, it was not appearing high enough in the search engine rankings. He brought in SEO agency Fresh Egg to address the situation and set the challenge of achieving at least 100 enquiries per day.

The agency decided that the best way to achieve this target was to ensure that Nationwide appeared above key competitors in search engine results pages – a serious challenge given the competitiveness of the vehicle leasing sector. So Fresh Egg got busy. The team redesigned and rebuilt the website and began an SEO campaign, improving and adding site content. This involved enhancing site architecture, implementing a link strategy, developing and maintaining a company blog, and creating a broader product offering to help capture the most diverse range of search terms possible.

The results have been impressive. No other competitor can match Nationwide Vehicle Contracts for online visibility: traffic is driven to the site from 35,000 different search terms a month. The company consistently ranks in the top 3–5 for a variety of generic search terms, such as 'leasing', 'contract hire', 'car leasing', 'van leasing' and 'car contract hire', and it ranks in the top five for a range of search terms using manufacturers' brand names, such as 'BMW leasing' and 'Mercedes contract hire'.

As a direct result of this SEO campaign, Nationwide Vehicle Contracts stopped its online paid-for advertising in December 2008, saving £300,000 per year. The company's gross profit for 2008 showed a 42 per cent increase. Online visitor enquiries now total 170–200 a day, up by an average of 93 per cent for the past year.

brilliant recap

1 Search is the best way to get people to visit your website.

2 You can improve your website's search engine rankings yourself – it is not as mysterious an art as it may appear.

3 Read current advice online from bloggers and from the search engines themselves.

4 Make your site easy to crawl, fill it with the right keywords and encourage links to your site.

5 Continually refine your campaign.

CHAPTER 4

Search engine marketing

'Getting information off the Internet is like taking a drink from a fire hydrant.'

Mitchell Kapoor

What we'll cover in this chapter

Search engine marketing (SEM), or paid-for search, is a quick way of driving traffic to your website and an important element of most successful online marketing programmes. However, get it wrong and it can rapidly become a way to lose a large amount of money. So in this chapter you will find:

- five steps to successful SEM;
- advice from search specialist Rob Pierre, whose company in 2009 found more than 1 million new customers for its clients;
- the story of how bookseller Blackwell increased its online revenue by 74 per cent in one year through SEM activity.

In 2000, search engines began allowing people to sponsor searches. Through this SEM, when someone used a search engine to find a website, paid-for advertisements appeared alongside the natural results. It revolutionised the world of marketing.

For the first time, marketers can pay to show ads only to people who are looking specifically for what the marketer wants to promote. Sure, they could already achieve this with SEO, but as we have just seen, SEO takes a long time and a significant time investment to produce results. With this new form of marketing you can set up a campaign and have highly targeted traffic arriving on your site within an hour. All you do is bid on certain words, then when someone searches using those words, your ad appears and if they click on the ad they arrive at your site and you pay the amount you bid.

Q How exactly does Google determine the order of sponsored searches?

A This is a question many marketers ask. It is one that no one – other than Google – knows the precise answer to. It depends on the amount you bid, the amount other advertisers bid and the 'quality score' of all ads that are shown for that particular search. That quality score is calculated by an algorithm Google keeps close to its chest. The truth is that the algorithm is so complex no one could hope to understand it, much less adapt their site accordingly. Historical click-through rates count, as does the relevance of the content on your site, so if you follow the advice in Chapter 3 on making your site crawlable, using relevant keywords and including links, it will stand you in good stead in sponsored search listings.

As you might imagine, SEM has proved phenomenally successful. Estimates of the size of the SEM industry vary but are all in the billions of pounds. Without doubt it makes a huge amount of money for the likes of Google. The meteoric rise of that company is clear proof of the potential of SEM.

This is not to say that you should do it instead of SEO – it is a good complement to SEO. Most marketers do it while they wait for their SEO campaigns to get up to speed, then continue to do it – albeit at a reduced level – once those longer-term search campaigns are producing results. If for any reason you need to increase the number of people visiting your site, you can always increase your spend on SEM.

This scalability is one of the aspects of SEM that has so appealed to marketers. They also like the speed with which they can set up campaigns and measure how well they are working. And, of course, they appreciate the way it produces qualified leads. However, what really excites most marketers about SEM is that they can transfer the risk of the campaign to the media owner. Rather than agreeing to pay for a page in a magazine, a run of direct mail inserts or even the services of a publicist and then hoping that the investment produces results, with SEM they pay only once they have achieved the results.

Five steps to successful SEM

Despite the many potential benefits of SEM it is important to remember that it is not risk free. In fact, get it wrong and you can lose a lot of money in a short time. Like every other form of marketing it requires careful planning and skilled execution. Follow these five steps to get started.

1 Be clear about your objectives

This is a form of advertising, but it is very different from all other types of advertising you may have done in the past. Crucially, it is not about building your brand; it is purely about generating leads. It gets your name out there, but you need to be aware that it offers nothing more than that.

it always helps to start with a clear target

So begin with a clear understanding of how SEM will fit into your overall marketing mix and, crucially, how many leads you want it to generate for you. You may come back and refine this figure, but it always helps to start with a clear target.

2 Build a suitable landing environment

There is little point spending money driving traffic to your site if those visitors are put off by what they find there. If necessary, go back to Chapter 2 on website building and ensure that your site is as engaging, navigable and relevant as it should be.

Maybe consider going further and building specific landing pages for this campaign. You may decide to promote a particular product or service through your SEM campaign, so ask whether you would achieve a higher conversion rate if potential customers clicked straight through to a page about that product or service rather than to your general homepage.

3 Get your words right

Bid on the right words and the right people will visit your site. It sounds so simple, but in fact it is a highly complex operation and the success of your SEM campaign hinges on you getting it exactly right. You need to know exactly who you want to attract to your site. You need to know precisely what words they are using. You need to know which words will bring you the wrong visitors. And you need to ensure you can get these words at the right price.

Fortunately, SEM is scalable and testable. So start small and grow your campaign. Think about the words your ideal customer might use. Look at what your competitors are doing. Use free tools such as Google AdWords. Aim to get a mix of exact words, which will produce a smaller number of highly qualified leads, and broad words, which will produce a larger number of less well-qualified visitors.

Think also about negative keywords. These are words which a large number of people will search for and where you might end up paying for click-throughs, but which will produce a majority of visitors with no interest in your products or services. For example, if you were the Apple store you would want to put 'vinegar' and 'cider' as negative keywords, otherwise a lot of people will arrive at your site hoping to find a speciality apple products site rather than wanting to buy an iPod, iMac or iPad.

4 Write ads that people will want to click on

You can improve the quality and quantity of your traffic, and so get a better return for your investment in SEM, by carefully considering your ad copy. You have very few words to explain to searchers what you sell, so ensure your copy is accurate, enticing and has a clear call to action.

5 Test, track, enhance

It is remarkable how many marketers set up SEM campaigns, then leave them for a month or even longer. Perhaps they remain stuck in traditional marketing methods. Perhaps they don't know just how trackable SEM is. Perhaps they simply have money to burn. Whatever the reason, they are making a mistake.

Within an hour of starting an SEM campaign you should have an initial idea of how well your keywords are performing. You may spot something that is producing a lot of irrelevant traffic, thus costing you money for no results. Drop it immediately. Within 24 hours you should be able to see which words are producing the most traffic and conversions. Focus your campaign in that direction. By spending some time every day testing, tracking and refining your campaign in this way, you can really make the most of this technique.

A great way to get started is to use Google Analytics. It is a free, detailed and incredibly useful tool that tells you how many people are visiting your site, where they are coming from and so on, and thus gives you invaluable information to improve your site.

Expert interview: **Rob Pierre, Managing Director, Jellyfish**

Rob Pierre first got into search marketing in 2005. He was working for a consultancy that provided IT support to fledgling websites such as that run by consumer advice publisher *Which?*. Following an article he read about a new form of marketing – SEM – Pierre and his colleagues proposed an SEM campaign. The client gave them a budget of £1,000 for an initial campaign. That produced a good return and the budget grew. Before he knew it, Pierre was working in the search marketing industry.

Today he runs Jellyfish, a global company of 80 people. It manages around 150 campaigns at any one time and in 2009 produced nearly 1 million customers for its publishing clients alone, such as the BBC, Dennis, EMAP, Haymarket and Reed. Even after a decade of phenomenal growth, the company continues to grow at around 20 per cent a year.

AB: It is fairly straightforward for companies to do their own marketing, isn't it? Why do so many of them choose to hire you?

RP: Yes, you can do SEM yourself, that's absolutely true. And if you're doing it for the first time I'd advise you to do exactly that. Familiarise yourself with how it all works. Just bid on a handful of keywords and monitor the results – keep a close eye on how much you're spending. You'll probably find it easier and more effective than you expect.

But you'll soon reach a point where the return you get for increased investment diminishes. You need to work harder and harder to get the right words, to appear above your competitors, to reach the promised land of the top left of the screen rather than the right-hand column. That's where you need to bring in the experts.

▶

You can't rely on an algorithm to do this – you need skilled specialists who can analyse your results and optimise your campaigns so you get the best results possible for the money you spend. You can do this yourself, but because we're doing it all day every day for 150 clients, we already know what works and what doesn't. We can save you a lot of time and make you a lot of money.

Finally, you also need someone who's on top of changes in the industry. For example, we can help you make the most of site links, whereby you can pay for up to four sub-links. We're also looking forward to making more and more use of semantic search, which is using a searcher's geography, history and even social media connections to inform a site. Keeping abreast of these important developments is time-consuming and difficult for a non-specialist.

 example

Blackwell

In 1995, bookseller Blackwell launched the first transactional online bookstore in the UK, giving people across the world access to more than 150,000 titles. In 2008 it redesigned its site and asked SEM agency Blue Barracuda to plan and manage an SEM campaign to deliver first, increased traffic to the site and second, increased online book sales.

Blue Barracuda planned a paid search campaign across Google, MSN and Yahoo! that would deliver maximum exposure of Blackwell's catalogue. It bid aggressively on volume categories, such as medical and law books, and supplemented this with specific campaigns around book titles and authors. To avoid cannibalising Blackwell's organic listings, the agency did not bid on brand terms.

The agency went back to the user testing carried out during the website redesign to ensure they had the right ad copy and landing pages. This involved research into the target audience of students, academics and educated professionals, including mapping the social media behaviour of university students to identify search patterns and terms.

Blue Barracuda reviews seasonality and trends to ensure the search budgets are allocated appropriately alongside automated techniques to ensure the warehouse stock level is reflected in the bid strategy. Clicks are weighted to ensure generic clicks receive the appropriate attribution for a sale and the agency integrates with Blackwell's other marketing activity, such as offline advertising.

In one year the SEM campaign delivered a significant increase in sales and a 74 per cent increase in revenue. In that time the cost-per-acquisition has fallen and the return on investment is almost double the target set by Blackwell. The SEM budget has consequently increased.

Jessica Armishaw, Head of Online Marketing at Blackwell, comments: 'Our ongoing search engine marketing enables us to expose our entire catalogue online without wasting any budget. Blackwell features in the right places on search engines so that students and academics can find the specific book they are seeking as well as books in their relevant categories. The activity also has a very positive effect on other aspects of the business, such as helping to manage stock levels.'

 **recap**

1 Search engine marketing is a quick way of driving traffic to your site. It is scalable and you pay only for results, so it is much lower risk than traditional forms of advertising.

2 However, get SEM wrong and you can pay too much money for the wrong sort of traffic.

3 Produce quality ads that will grab people's attention and make them want to click through to your site.

4 Follow the advice on search engine optimisation to ensure that your paid-for ad appears high on the sponsored search listings.

5 Ensure your landing environment converts this traffic into sales.

CHAPTER 5

Online
advertising

'You can fool all the people all the
time if the advertising is right and
the budget is big enough.'

Joseph E. Levine

What we'll cover in this chapter

With 60 per cent of UK population now going online at least once a day, it is little wonder that UK advertisers spend more than £3.5 billion on online ads every year. In this chapter you will find:

- advice on how to buy the right space online;
- details of how seed producer Suttons Seeds works closely with online publishers to run a successful online advertising programme;
- advice on how to produce ads that use that space most effectively;
- the views of Richard Sharp, one of the UK's leading online advertising experts, on how to get the most out of this fast-changing medium;
- the story of how nursery and baby supplier Kiddicare improved its online ads and so increased its online sales by 146 per cent in a year;
- an interview with online voucher expert Guy Keeling;
- a look at the online advertising done by chocolate retailer Hotel Chocolat.

In the first half of 2009 the Internet overtook television to become the UK's single biggest advertising medium. Although most of the advertising industry knew it was only a matter of time before it happened, the announcement in September that year from the Internet Advertising Bureau (IAB) still made many sit up and take notice.

The IAB's six-monthly report, conducted in association with PricewaterhouseCoopers and the World Advertising Research Centre, revealed that while spending on advertising as a whole had fallen by 16.6

per cent, online advertising spend was actually up by 4.6 per cent. So, not only was it taking the place of traditional advertising techniques, online advertising was even defying the worst recession in living memory.

There are many reasons why, at the time of writing, UK advertisers were spending more than £3.5 billion on online advertising. The first is that, quite simply, that is where the audience is. Where once there were three or four television channels and prime-time audiences were regularly above 10 million, now the television audience is split between hundreds of channels and people are spending more time online.

We live ever more of our lives on the Internet. We buy our groceries, chat with our friends, pay our bills and follow the football scores online. Five years ago using the Internet might have added to the way we lived our lives; now it is the way we live our lives. It is not only television that has suffered as a result. Marketers in every part of the country and in every sector have diverted advertising spend away from radio, posters, newspapers and magazines as increasingly the audience shifts online. For that reason alone, the Internet is no longer a medium that an advertiser can ignore.

> we live ever more of our lives on the Internet

There are many other reasons for the meteoric rise of online advertising, though. One is cost. Without the high production costs of broadcast or print media, website owners have been able to dramatically undercut their offline rivals. Perhaps more importantly, however, they have also adopted performance-based payment models. Where traditionally advertisers would pay to rent column inches, airtime or a poster site for a certain amount of time, with online advertising that operates payment for performance, they pay only if they get the desired result, be that a click to their website, completion of a brochure request or an actual sale.

This has revolutionised the advertising industry. It was John Wanamaker, a 20th-century American businessman, religious leader and politician, who famously said: 'Half the money I spend on advertising is wasted; the trouble is I don't know which half.' The performance-based payment model has eliminated this perennial problem for the advertiser. Now not one penny of the money you spend on advertising need be wasted.

In the same way, you can gather a vast amount of data about the people who view or click on your ad. This allows advertisers to build sharper profiles of their customers and so refine not only their advertising but even their products and services. It is the sort of targeted marketing and feedback that marketers 20 years ago could only dream of.

Yet, despite this host of compelling reasons to advertise online, and despite the overwhelming evidence to suggest that UK advertisers are becoming more enthusiastic, there are still a great many people who shy away from online advertising. Many are confused by what is an undeniably complex array of publishers, networks, affiliates, optimisers, exchanges, agencies and so on. Others feel ill-equipped to produce the right creative.

In many ways they are right to approach online advertising with caution. Poorly funded and naively produced ads can damage a brand. One of the great strengths of the Internet as a marketing medium is that your messages can go viral, which means that people can send your ads between each other at the click of a button, potentially spreading your ad to millions and millions of people in a matter of days. It's a great thing if those viewers are admiring your work, less so if they are mocking it.

In this chapter we will look at how to buy the right space, how to produce the right creative and how to devise and run a successful campaign.

How to buy the right space

Broadly speaking, you have three options for where you place your ads. You can go directly to a website owner. If you know exactly who you want to reach and there is a site that reaches those people, this can be the simplest and most effective approach. It is also the best way to get the premium space. However, you pay for that privilege.

If you have a more dispersed target audience or you are happy to accept the space that the publishers have been unable to sell directly to advertisers, you might want to consider exchanges or networks. The main ad exchanges are Microsoft's AdECN, Yahoo!'s Right Media and Google's DoubleClick, and they all offer something slightly different, but in essence they are technology platforms that you buy and then use to bid for online advertising space. Because you manage the process yourself, these exchanges are a relatively inexpensive way to access a global community of publishers across a vast array of topics, meaning that your advertising is more likely to appear in the place where your potential customers are. You can also get some fairly sophisticated information on how well your ads are performing on different sites and in different markets, allowing you to optimise your campaigns. A growing number of marketers are beginning to enhance their performance on ad networks by investing in automated bidding software or even agencies that manage their presence and ensure they pick up the best space.

For more sophisticated targeting and analysis, though, you need to go to the networks. These are essentially more sophisticated and expensive exchanges. The team of people at the network do all the work for you, so they cost more, but they promise better targeting, higher-value space and improved results. There are more than 100 ad networks in the UK, ranging from niche networks that promise highly targeted campaigns in a given sector or interest group, such as *The Guardian's* Green Ad Network, through to generalised networks that promise broader reach. In order to optimise your campaigns some of these networks employ teams of technical experts or they have developed clever software that can do it automatically.

The early networks were blind, meaning that advertisers had little idea where their ads were placed and this led to several instances of brands finding their ads in entirely inappropriate places. This caused major damage to the ad network industry. It responded by introducing a code of conduct policed by industry body Internet Advertising Sales Houses (IASH). In addition, many networks are now transparent so you can see exactly where your ads are appearing.

The online advertising market is indeed complex. It is becoming even more complex with the arrival of demand-side platforms, which are networks of advertisers, and publisher yield optimisers, which are intermediaries who interrogate data to enhance ad results across the inventories of their client publishers. The advertiser finding their feet in the online advertising world should be able to ignore these new arrivals for now – it is a complex enough area already.

Most advertisers end up with a combination of direct purchases and either an exchange or a network. However, be wary of rushing in too quickly. While pay-per-performance models can be a great way to ensure you pay only for the outcomes you want, if you define those desired outcomes poorly, or you structure a deal in the wrong way, they can also be a great way to lose a lot of money very quickly.

Whichever route you choose to go down, think carefully about who you want to reach, what you want to say to them and the outcomes that you are willing to pay for. Then begin small. Start with a low-level campaign in a niche area and agree a limit on how much you will spend in a given time period. Carefully monitor results. Once you have a model that is working, only then begin to invest more heavily in it.

Bear in mind also that it usually pays dividends to invest time in nurturing your relationship with your publisher. This is especially true when you are using a network of publishers. The prime sites can pick the advertisers they think will generate the most revenue, so you need to keep them constantly updated with news on your campaigns, offers and products.

 example

Suttons Seeds

Founded in 1806, seed retailer Suttons Seeds receives more than 75,000 unique visitors to its website annually. It has built much of this traffic through its relationship with affiliate network Webgains. Brian O'Donnell, E-Commerce Manager, believes that key to this success has been the relationship the company develops with its affiliates. He explains: 'We make sure we give our affiliates the best products and tools to work with, such as communicating the latest offers and providing good product data feeds. We keep an open channel of communication and take regular feedback from our affiliates. The good sites have the pick of advertisers, so it really pays to put in this effort.'

Even when you are buying directly from a site you should liaise frequently with the team there so you have a good understanding of the content they are producing, how it sits with your ad creative, what type of visitor it is attracting and what technical development plans they have for the future that you might be able to take advantage of.

Seven steps to making the most of the space you buy

The space you buy for your advertising is important, but it is not the only factor that will determine whether or not your campaign succeeds. In fact, one of the greatest mistakes many marketers make with online advertising – indeed with offline advertising as well – is spending all the money on the media space and allocating too small a budget to producing a good ad.

> you need to produce an ad that will resonate with your audience

In order to get the greatest value out of the space you have bought, you need to produce an ad that will resonate with your audience, that compels them to act and that results in the outcomes you want. Follow these seven steps to ensure you achieve all of that.

1 Know what you want to achieve

Any sensible planning process must always begin with clarity on the objectives you want to achieve. If you are vague about your desired outcomes, your campaign will never be a success. Regardless of what you achieve you will always be left with the feeling that you could have achieved more. So, pin down these objectives very precisely. What will success look like? Is it an increase in sales? A growth in the number of leads you pass to the sales department? An uplift in the number of visitors to your website? Or something else?

Put actual numbers and deadlines to these targets. It should be a 10 per cent sales increase by the end of the year, or 100 new leads for the sales team in the first three months, or doubling the number of website visitors in 12 months.

2 Understand your audience

If you are going to produce an ad that grabs the attention of your target audience and inspires them to act, you need to have a good understanding of that target audience. What sort of person is going to see this ad? What issues do they face? What excites them?

Don't assume you know the answers to all this. Invest time and, if necessary, money in research to get accurate and up-to-date answers to these questions. This can be as sophisticated as hiring market research special-ists to conduct focus groups or as simple as visiting a trade show and talking to a few potential customers.

3 Refine your message

Your next step is to adapt your marketing message to give them some-thing that will excite them. Ideally, this will be a clear, simple message. If the message is confusing then potential customers are less likely to click through and complete the desired result of the campaign.

Find something in your products or your services that will appeal to this specific audience and then put that to them clearly and simply. It could be a product feature, a service differentiator or even a marketing incentive, such as a discount – whatever it is, it needs to stand out from the thou-sands of other marketing messages that your audience will receive that day.

4 Select the right format

Not so long ago the only option for your online ad was a small banner ad. They had fewer animation possibilities than an e-mail, so it was little wonder that many of the early advertisers on the Web quickly became disillusioned and stopped advertising. Now, though, there are many more possibilities. From much larger banner ads to overlay ads and user-initiated rich media, there is much that you can do to bring your creative and your message to life.

Bear in mind, however, that just because these techniques exist, you do not have to use them. Ensure that your audience does not find them intru-sive and always ask yourself what the format is adding to the campaign.

5 Invest in quality creative

Never assume that just because your ad is in the right place, uses the ideal format and contains a compelling message your audience will look at it, much less click on it. You need to invest in high-quality creative and that might well involve hiring specialists. We are not just talking production values here, although you want to ensure that text is format-ted correctly, that sound is clear and pictures look professional. It is just as important that your ad is constructed to pique the audience's interest quickly, that you don't make the common mistake of trying to tell a 30-second story with your ad. Web viewers will simply look away before the end.

Advertising professionals are used to creating 'stoppers' (images or words that make people take notice of the ad) for posters and other traditional media and they can apply these techniques to your online campaign to create a campaign with genuine stand-out.

6 Build a landing page that works

Once people have clicked on your ad they need to be taken straight to a landing page that relates to what they have clicked on and guides them in the direction that you and they want to go. This destination page should also be simple and easy to use.

7 Integrate, monitor, enhance

Finally, as with all online marketing, integrate your display advertising with the online and offline marketing plan. Remember to track the performance of your campaign and to adapt it over time. Online is about constant improvement.

Expert interview: **Richard Sharp, Director of Media and Head of Trading, ValueClick in the UK**

Richard Sharp joined ValueClick, one of the UK's largest and most long-standing ad networks, in January 2007. Before then he had worked as Head of Retail at Hemscott Plc and Head of Agency Sales at the Financial Times UK. He has since been elected to chair IASH, the organisation within the IAB set up to help to police the display advertising industry to protect both brands and consumers. Over the past ten years he has witnessed and played a part in some incredible developments and changes to the online advertising industry.

AB: So, it's pretty widely known that more and more marketers are choosing to spend their money online. Why is that? What's so appealing about online advertising?

RS: Ultimately, online is a channel that is underpinned by performance. The nature of the channel means that it can be tracked and optimised throughout the campaign to ensure it is performing at its best and achieving top results. That's what makes online advertising unique. There are several optimisation and retargeting techniques that can be applied to any campaign, depending on what the objectives of the campaign and business are.

AB: I agree that the potential of online advertising is enormous. But it's also incredibly confusing for anyone who doesn't work in the area. Can you tell my readers, in simple terms, exactly how it all works?

RS: The first step is for the advertiser to define campaign objectives with our sales team. We will then determine the best payment model for the campaign. It may be that the advertiser is best paying per thousand viewers of his ad, or per click on the ad, or for each new customer it acquires through the campaign.

AB: And how do they know that you'll pick the best one for them?

RS: Because we want the return on their investment to be as high as possible. That way we make more money from their campaign and also they're more likely to come back and spend even more on our network.

AB: OK. What next?

RS: Next, our operations team will upload the different adverts. They could be any type of format the advertiser wants.

AB: The advertiser needs to produce these himself?

RS: Yes. Our job is then to push those ads out across our network of IASH-approved sites and to monitor and optimise the campaign.

AB: How exactly do you do that?

RS: Partly technology, which allows us to target people based on geography and behaviour, and partly an operations team, which is constantly tracking the campaign's performance. We also have a team behind the scenes that continually monitors sites to ensure that there isn't any illegal activity occurring. At the end of the campaign, reports are generated to analyse performance.

AB: Geographical targeting I can understand – you know where someone is so you serve them an ad based on that – but what is behavioural targeting and how does it work?

▶

RS: It's a really exciting and fast-developing aspect of online advertising. It's all about targeting consumers through their behaviour online. It can be through retargeting them with new offers when they click out of a site, thereby enticing them back to the same product with a new offer. Or it can be through predicting the kinds of advertising they would like to see by tracking their IP addresses and looking for trends in their viewing habits. For example, someone who visits a variety of cooking sites is likely to respond positively to advertising for the latest cookbook. The important thing with behavioural targeting is to ensure that users are not spooked out by the concept. This means we need to educate them on the advantages of this technology and explain to them that no personally identifiable information is tracked.

AB: So what else is new and exciting in this area?

RS: Advertising using video and mobile phones is still very new and looks set to develop over the next few years. Consumer adoption of the iPhone and other smartphones is likely to play an increased role in its development.

AB: What of the future? What will we see coming through in the next year or two?

RS: I think we will see more advertisers using online advertising for brand building. To date the thinking has been that online is good for customer acquisition, but you reserve your bigger brand-building budgets for offline channels. I think that's changing and will continue to change in the next couple of years. All this will mean that advertising on television and radio, and especially in magazines, will continue to decline, whereas online ad spend will continue to increase.

AB: Finally, what advice would you offer my readers on how to get their online advertising right?

RS: I've got two pieces of advice. Firstly, don't forget that display advertising is just one area of online marketing. Far too many companies bolt it on to the end of a campaign rather than using it as the foundation for a broader range of online marketing activities. Secondly, don't make the mistake of approaching it like an offline advertising campaign, of producing your ads, buying the space and then waiting for the results to roll in. The great strength of online advertising is that you can monitor results and so adapt performance – but it's only a strength if you use it.

 **example**

Kiddicare

Established in 1974, Kiddicare describes itself as the largest privately owned nursery and baby supplier in the UK. Its 60,000 square foot showroom in Peterborough is one of the largest baby retail spaces in Europe. The family-run business prides itself on its customer service and its next-day delivery promise.

While this extensive product range and focus on customer service was generating orders from more than 400,000 customers a year, Kiddicare wanted to increase its sales by making better use of affiliates and it saw online advertising through affiliates as the best way to achieve this. As part of this campaign it was also keen to increase co-ordination between its different online marketing channels in order to accurately measure the effectiveness of each and their impact on each other. So it brought digital agency Blue Barracuda on board to re-energise the company's online advertising. Martin Talks, CEO of Blue Barracuda, says: 'We wanted to increase the effectiveness of the affiliate marketing campaign and take a more strategic approach to complement the company's search engine marketing.'

The first step was to start working more closely with the publishers who were running Kiddicare's ads on their sites. The company began sending them a weekly newsletter detailing new products, promotions and other relevant company news. It also invested in the account management team so that there was more one-to-one contact with those publishers. This not only increased publisher enthusiasm for Kiddicare ads, it also gave the company a clearer view of which publisher sites and which campaigns produced the best results.

It deployed de-duping technology and local cookie tracking across the programme to ensure activity from the different affiliate segments was correctly attributed. This reduced costs, so the budget could be more effectively deployed. It also allowed for deeper analysis of the affiliate segments which worked most effectively and their impact on each other. Testing could be implemented on different segments and alternative strategies adopted each month.

Armed with this information, Blue Barracuda was able to extend Kiddicare's affiliate programme. It added a third affiliate network and new types of affiliate, such as incentive sites, cashback sites and voucher sites. The results from this activity were impressive. The overall number of clicks on Kiddicare's ads in 2009 more than doubled compared with 2008. Sales value increased by 146 per cent.

Expert interview: Guy Keeling, Managing Director, Maximiles UK

Affiliate marketing is often associated only with online advertising. However, much affiliate marketing goes on offline and has done for decades. Furthermore, there is a significant amount of online affiliate marketing that is not pure advertising. A growing proportion of this is online vouchers and coupons. Here, Guy Keeling, MD of online loyalty company Maximiles UK, explains how this area works, why you should be interested and how to make it work as well as possible for your products and company.

AB: Hi Guy. Tell us a bit about yourself.

GK: I have over ten years' experience in loyalty programmes and affiliate marketing, having worked as head of consumer markets at Dunnhumby, heading up Tesco Clubcard. I also sit on the board of the Internet Advertising Bureau's Affiliate Marketing Council.

AB: And what about your company?

GK: Maximiles is the European leader in online loyalty services. We've been operating for the past ten years across Europe, working with major brands to drive sales through loyalty marketing, market research and digital direct marketing services. In the UK, Maximiles also operates its own loyalty service.

AB: So, why should readers be interested in online vouchers?

GK: It's the logical step for consumer brands seeking the best use for strained marketing budgets, as the cash-savvy consumer turns to online shopping, price comparison, loyalty and cash-back programmes to ensure they are rewarded for parting with their hard-earned cash. We've got a list of 600 partners and affiliates on Maximiles, all of whom have brands that are interested in offering their products through our own loyalty portal or looking to create their own online loyalty scheme.

AB: How does it work?

GK: Essentially, the affiliate site offers good deals to consumers and so encourages traffic to advertisers' sites. As with online advertising through affiliates, they take a percentage of all resulting sales.

AB: And what form can those good deals take?

GK: There are many options: comparison shopping websites and directories, loyalty websites which provide points or cash back for purchases, voucher coupon websites and so on.

AB: Which is the best approach?

GK: Presenting daily rewards or opportunities for cash back provides an incentive for saving up for a bigger reward and encourages consumers to develop loyalty to specific online retailers, which is something that has traditionally been fairly difficult to maintain.

AB: What about vouchers?

GK: Increasingly, voucher codes are forming part of the affiliate marketing mix, as brands try to tempt shoppers with special promotions and limited time offers. These are very useful for driving considerable interest in something in a short time span. However, the IAB Affiliate Marketing Council has recently strengthened guidelines on voucher codes, following complaints about companies issuing expired vouchers and promoting misleading special offers. Herein lies the problem with voucher codes: even with the best intentions, it is not possible to guarantee consumers they are getting the best deal by using voucher codes for discounts. Shopping around through comparison sites and eBay could actually result in better value.

This is why I believe loyalty and cash-back programmes tend to be a better option. Not only do they save consumers more money, so encouraging greater loyalty, but they also present marketers with greater data-gathering opportunities. You can collect transactional and behavioural data and then use this to implement tactical campaigns to drive desired behaviours, something that would otherwise be difficult to achieve through either search or display advertising.

AB: How should a marketer go about getting started in this area?

GK: The key is to understand who you are targeting and to offer them something that will appeal to them. There is no point whatsoever in offering a deal which is totally irrelevant to the site where it is positioned or the people to whom it is emailed.

AB: Any other advice?

GK: Don't be afraid of offering incentives. Consumers are getting savvier and they know that they can probably find a good deal from a competitor if

▶

the rewards aren't good enough. Points, free goods or cash back all help incentivise a sale. Finally, keep an eye on cost-per-order ratios. While voucher codes can encourage sales, they won't necessarily provide the greatest profit. By contrast, encouraging consumers to buy goods at full price in exchange for points to be redeemed at a later date can provide a far better return on investment.

AB: What's new and cutting edge in this area?

GK: Increasingly, marketers are looking to engage consumers by asking them to complete surveys online. In the longer term, we will see the development of online R&D panels, targeting shoppers with samples of products to help market research and keeping online diaries and blogs of their product use.

At present we have over 1.5 million people registered to complete surveys and 250,000 who complete them regularly; this is a huge consumer base for brands. These are people who are not professional survey-fillers but rather members of the public who have been incentivised to fill in some information. This base can be reached quickly – often a survey can be turned around within 24 hours – and is wholly representative of UK adults. Given that it is becoming increasingly difficult to extract information from an adult population that is bombarded with surveys and marketing, the use of loyalty and affiliate programmes stands out as a great way to conduct all-important market research.

AB: What of the future?

GK: Online loyalty marketing is really only in its infancy. I fully expect the practice to grow and develop as more marketers realise the potential there is here. Each successive Bellwether Report shows ad spend dwindling, so the future lies with the more youthful marketing channels, such as online vouchers.

This will create far greater competition in this area. Loyalty marketing is well established offline – just look at the popularity of store cards – but it is just finding its feet online. I predict that more and more brands will either join or create their own online loyalty platform. Ultimately, the level of brand engagement which it offers means that brands cannot afford to ignore this means of marketing for much longer.

 **example**

Hotel Chocolat

Established in 1994, Hotel Chocolat was launched with one goal in mind: 'To make a better type of chocolate available to UK consumers bored by the mediocrity of that available in supermarkets and on the high street.' Now, Hotel Chocolat is a leading international chocolate retailer online, via catalogue and in more than 40 stores on the UK high street.

Retail Week awarded the company its Emerging Retailer of the Year award in 2007 and in September of that year the company expanded into the US with the launch of its American website, followed shortly afterwards by the opening of two stores in Boston in 2009.

Hotel Chocolat's peak sales periods are seasonal and predominately around the times of the year when people tend to give each other presents. In 2008 an early Easter meant that the company's biggest sales events – Christmas, Valentine's Day, Mother's Day and Easter – all occurred within a four-month period.

Matthew Keys, Online Commercial Development Executive at Hotel Chocolat, recalls: 'During those four busy trading months for the company alongside the launch of our American business we needed an online advertising programme that was both efficient and effective.'

To provide this boost to its advertising the company worked closely with online advertising network Commission Junction. Keys explains why: 'We chose Commission Junction because it has extensive experience in the retail space both here in the UK and internationally. This gave us confidence that we would be able to achieve our ambitious goals.'

In the first quarter of 2008 Hotel Chocolat saw online sales rise by 21 per cent from the first quarter of 2007 and Keys attributes a high proportion of this growth to the work done with Commission Junction. However, while the experience and the sheer scale that Commission Junction brought to the campaign were undoubtedly important, this campaign also demonstrates the importance of advertisers working closely with publishers.

Hotel Chocolat puts its publisher affiliates in bronze, silver and gold tiers, awarding higher commission percentages for those in the higher tiers. This ensures that during the peak periods, such as the first quarter of 2008, those affiliates remain incentivised to run Hotel Chocolat ads rather than those of the company's competitors.

Hotel Chocolat also provided a whole range of information and creative to different parts of its audience. It ran a blog, as well as audio and video podcasts, specifically for its affiliates and even provided product training to some affiliates. Finally, the team at Hotel Chocolat were active on the affiliate forums and were always open and available to affiliates.

It was this ongoing commitment to building strong relationships with affiliates and rewarding the publishers who achieved sales for the company that produced such an impressive surge in online sales, got the new US site off to a strong start and laid the foundations for productive online advertising for many years to come.

 **recap**

1 Online advertising is now more popular with marketers than television advertising.

2 This is for several reasons: more people are spending more time online; online advertising is often more affordable than offline equivalents; online advertising is less risky and more scalable.

3 You can buy space either directly or through an intermediary; whichever route you choose, you should try to build long-term constructive relationships with your publishing partners.

4 Invest in ad copy to ensure you hit the right people with the right message at the right time.

5 The use of online vouchers and coupons is an increasingly popular way of getting the attention of potential customers, so consider this option.

CHAPTER 6

E-mail marketing

'Diamonds are for ever;
e-mail comes close.'

June Kronholz

What we'll cover in this chapter

E-mail marketing has become one of the most effective and popular forms of marketing. In this chapter you will find:

- 12 steps to successful e-mail marketing;
- an in-depth look at the past, present and future of e-mail marketing by Ian Hitt;
- the story of how airline Icelandair used e-mail marketing to increase online sales by 160 per cent in a year.

No other form of marketing consistently produces as good a return on investment as e-mail marketing. The Direct Marketing Association (DMA) in the US produced a 2009 report, 'The power of direct', which revealed that in 2009 for every $1 spent on e-mail marketing the return was $43.62.

For several years some observers have predicted that e-mail is losing its efficacy and it is indeed true that return on investment in e-mail marketing is falling – in 2008 it was $44.93 for every $1 spent and in 2010 it was predicted to be $42.08 for every $1 spent – but the return is still remarkably high. For the sake of comparison, the next best return in the DMA report came from online search, which produced a return of $21.85 for each $1 spent.

Not only is e-mail marketing one of the most effective forms of online marketing, it is also one of the most popular. According to Forrester Research, the European email marketing sector will grow to be worth £2.15 billion by 2012.

Every business has e-mail, so even if you do no more than include your switchboard number at the bottom of your e-mails, you are to a small extent using e-mail for marketing. There is, of course, much more that you can do. Some businesses use e-mail to welcome new subscribers or shoppers. Others use it to reinvigorate shoppers who have abandoned online shopping carts or to inform customers of despatch and delivery dates. Some send regular newsletters updating subscribers on promotions, new products, company news and so on. Business-to-business (B2B) companies use these newsletters to promote seminars, research papers, etc.

Like so much online marketing, e-mail is a great leveller. Do an online search for 'e-mail marketing provider' and you will find several sites where you can devise and send an e-mail marketing campaign in just hours for much less than £100. You may be a one-person online-only retailer, but your e-mails will arrive in the inbox next to those of Tesco and John Lewis.

You can also specifically target and personalise your messages with e-mail. It is possible to segment your target audience by geography, age or demographic group. Then you can break it down further by what they have bought in the past or how they have responded to previous marketing communications. Once you have done that you can personalise the communications, not only addressing recipients by name but by presenting offers that you know are likely to appeal to them or giving them information that you know will interest them.

What is more, you will be able to use fairly sophisticated tracking tools to see – within minutes of sending – how many of those e-mails were opened, how many recipients clicked on links and so on. This allows you to immediately adapt your campaign, focusing your efforts on what works and abandoning what doesn't.

Compare that to the direct marketing campaigns of yesteryear, where it was punitively expensive to segment by anything more than the simplest geo-demographics, and where we had to wait weeks or months to get any indication of which target segment, which message and which creative treatment was most successful, and you begin to see just why marketers have embraced e-mail so enthusiastically over the past decade.

This channel is not going away. Some have predicted that it will be sidelined by the emergence of social media such as Facebook, Twitter and LinkedIn, but according to a survey conducted in 2009 by e-Dialog International, only 2 per cent of respondents between the ages of 18 and 24 prefer to be contacted about new products via social networks. This compares with 66 per cent who prefer to be contacted via e-mail. Furthermore, in the same age group, 62 per cent said they are more likely to make a purchase online after receiving a promotion e-mail, compared with only 24 per cent if the same communication was made via social media. This clearly shows that e-mail is strongly recognised as the appropriate channel for commercial communication.

However, despite the enormous potential of this medium, far too few companies make the most of it. Too often companies see it as just a cheap and easy alternative to direct mail. They cobble together a list of e-mail addresses, instruct the office junior to knock together an e-mail and then blast it out. If they don't get enough responses, they just fire it off again. The problem is that if they do this to enough e-mail addresses enough times, they probably will get a few responses and this persuades them to see this approach as successful. They ignore the damage they do to their reputation in the eyes of all those who see them as little more than spammers, and crucially, they miss out on the full potential of this medium.

brilliant definition

Spam is the sending of a large quantity of marketing messages to a random group of people. It is estimated that it makes up more than 80 per cent of all e-mail sent. It is illegal in many parts of the world.

12 steps to succeeding at e-mail marketing

It is easy to do e-mail marketing; it is difficult to do it well. The chances are that, like many companies, you have done some sort of e-mail marketing in the past and that, like many companies, you feel you could do it better.

The principles are simple – build a list of prospective customers and e-mail them a marketing message – but as you may have found, people are increasingly immune to marketing messages arriving in their in-box. While that approach to e-mail marketing may have worked a few years ago and may still produce some small return, you will find it increasingly difficult to make any serious headway without introducing some sophistication to your e-mail marketing campaigns. Following are 12 ways you can improve your e-mail marketing campaigns.

 **timesaver**

To transform an e-mail marketing campaign overnight is a significant undertaking. It may seem like too much to do in one go. Not only do you need to find the time and possibly money to invest in it, you also need to persuade colleagues that the return is worth the effort. So, don't try. Instead, plan to introduce just one of the 12 elements outlined here every month for the next year. Do that and watch your open rates, click-through rates, response rates and sales soar. You will also find your colleagues becoming increasingly enthusiastic about your innovations.

1 Clean up your data

Data quality is the foundation of every successful e-mail marketing campaign. Sending e-mails to incorrect addresses or to people who have moved home, changed job or passed away is inefficient, so before you do anything else, make a concerted effort to clean up your data. Work out the best way of getting accurate names and addresses for all prospects on your list and then invest time in getting the list up to scratch.

At the same time, ensure you don't pollute your database with addresses you buy in. Make sure you know the opt-in policies of those putting it together. A slip-up here can result in you being blacklisted by a potential customer. Know how old the list is so you don't end up with a list that is cluttered with invalid e-mail addresses that would increase bouncebacks. Also be aware of when it was last mailed. Over-mail a list and you could be blacklisted by Internet service providers (ISPs).

2 Put in place a system for collecting e-mail addresses

Very often businesses spend large amounts of money buying in data from external sources and neglect the swathes of data they already hold or which they could collect in the course of their everyday activities. Devise a system to collect e-mail addresses at every single point your business interacts with a customer or prospect. This could be on your website, at the point of sale, via a call centre, at exhibitions, through surveys, and so on. Consider providing a financial incentive to your staff for their contribution in building this database. However, be careful to put in place a system for protecting the quality of your data. You may need to appoint a data quality champion to police inputs, or even better develop a culture whereby staff in all departments understand the value of a well-maintained email marketing database.

consider providing a financial incentive to your staff

3 Be spot on with your opt-ins

Everyone knows that there are stringent rules surrounding what you can and cannot do with marketing data. However, not everyone is so sure about exactly what those rules are and even fewer still actually make sure they follow them. If you want to avoid the possibility of damaging fines and the likelihood of alienating your prospects, you should aim to be in that select few who understand and comply with the law in this area. The Direct Marketing Association E-mail Marketing Council produces Best Practice Guidelines which should help to steer you through these waters. Visit www.dma.org.uk.

However, you should aim to go beyond this basic legal requirement and gain genuine opt-in from those who receive your e-mails. Let people know exactly what they will receive from you and how often. Give them the chance to alter this very easily. Provide an unsubscribe process which is clear, easy and fail-safe. Do this and you will rapidly achieve greater response to, and engagement with, your e-mails.

4 Grab attention with your subject line

Research has shown that most consumers base their decision to open an e-mail on the first 45 or so characters of its subject line. Word choice and word order are also key factors. Shorter is better, although targeted or niche audience e-mails can be exceptions to this rule. This is not just because time-poor consumers and business buyers want subject lines that match their attention spans but because some e-mail service providers display only the first 38–47 characters of a subject line in a recipient's in-box. Mobile devices display even less of the subject line. So consider your subject line carefully, test repeatedly and rewrite.

5 Deliver relevant content

Irrelevancy is the new spam. It takes only a few badly targeted and badly personalised e-mails for a prospect to start ignoring your e-mails. By targeting and personalising as much as possible – by thinking about those on your database as individuals rather than an amorphous lump of addresses to which you can blast out a single message – you will make huge improvements to your campaigns.

You can do this in several ways. You can ask for profile and preference information when people sign up and opt in. You can look at purchase data, both online and offline. You can look at your analytics package to see which e-mails they have responded to and what in those e-mails specifically has prompted action. Finally, you can look at their activity on your website. Which pages have they viewed, where have they clicked, what comments have they left? All of this information should help you to build up a picture of the individuals who are receiving your e-mails and what interests those individuals. Use the information to personalise your communications as specifically as you can afford to.

6 Use the medium to full advantage

One of the greatest dangers with e-mail marketing is thinking of it as just a letter without a stamp. Look at the last e-mail campaign you sent. What could you have done to make it more effective, to use the medium to greater effect? Does the e-mail link to your website? Does the reader have to scroll down to get to the offer or is it immediately obvious? Eye-tracking studies show that 60 per cent of readers make it to the bottom of those e-mails with images, so many marketers are introducing images and video to their e-mail campaigns.

7 Work out the best time to send your e-mails

You probably think you know the best time of day and week to send your emails, but 2009 research by e-mail marketing provider Pure360 produced some interesting facts that may make you question how you have approached this in the past.

Pure360 analysed more than 660,000 e-mails sent by 34 companies and discovered that, contrary to popular assumptions, the volume of marketing e-mails opened drops markedly during the lunch hour. A mere 9 per cent of the e-mails sent were opened between noon and 2pm, with 62 per cent of those opened being news or magazine alerts rather than promotions on goods or services.

Using the research, Pure360's team have identified patterns in consumers' responses to different e-mail marketing promotions throughout the day:

- The Abyss (10pm to 9am) – the worst time to send e-mail.
- Consumer AM (9am to 10am) – surprisingly, this was the second best time for e-mail opening, with consumers allowing themselves to be distracted by offers on clothes, live events, restaurants and consumer goods.
- Do Not Disturb (10am to noon) – consumers are not opening marketing e-mails, choosing instead to focus on work.
- The Lunchtime News (noon to 2pm) – counter-intuitively, consumers are also unlikely to open marketing e-mails during their lunch, choosing instead to spend time on news and magazine alerts.
- In The Zone (2pm to 3pm) – in the immediate post-lunch period consumers remain focused on work, responding only to e-mail offers relating to financial services.
- A Life-changing Afternoon (3pm to 5pm) – job-related apathy sets in and consumers start thinking about their personal situation, making this a good time for e-mails about property and financial services.

- Working Late (5pm to 7pm) – there is a dramatic rise in recipients opening holiday promotions during this period; it is also when business buyers have time to find out about B2B promotions.
- Last Orders (7pm to 10pm) – recipients are more likely to respond to consumer promotions in their own time; offers on clothes and special interests such as sports and gym promotions perform extremely well in this period.

8 Ensure your e-mails are delivered

E-mail delivery rates directly affect the success of e-mail marketing campaigns and are fast becoming a standard metric alongside click-through and open rates, the latter of which have become increasingly difficult to track accurately. So you should ensure that your e-mail service provider enjoys a good reputation with the ISP. Ask to see statistics on delivery rates broken down by ISP. Ask how many people they have allocated to ISP relations.

9 Open up a dialogue

One of the most appealing features of e-mail is that it allows a dialogue. You can spark a conversation with a prospect and thus engage them in a way that is impossible with print advertising or even traditional direct mail. Yet it is remarkable how many promotional e-mails explicitly discourage recipients from responding. In your next campaign, encourage recipients to respond. Ask for their views on a subject. Lead them to think of you as more than a faceless machine pumping marketing messages at them – let them interact with you and watch the impact on your open, click-through and response rates.

One of the most popular ways to encourage recipient engagement with e-mail is to ask people to cast their votes in a poll. It is popular because it works. Allow recipients to cast their votes with a simple click within the e-mail, then take them to your website to show them the current state of voting and from there lead them deeper into your site.

10 Do more than just promote

In the same way, do more than just send recipients a series of promotional messages. Instead, offer an unexpected free service, give them some information or even some entertainment. Not only do customers appreciate this form of communication more than direct selling, they respond better to it. Greater interactivity translates into higher open rates, increased brand advocacy and ultimately increased revenue. In brief, think partner, not prospect.

11 Piggyback your messages

If, having made all these changes, you are still struggling to improve your response rates, you might have to accept that you are trying to reach an audience that, for one reason or another, has switched off to your messages. You are not alone. The in-box is an increasingly busy place and marketers are all having to work harder to be heard.

Another tactic you could try is to stop sending marketing e-mails per se and instead include your marketing messages in other e-mails. These could be communications your organisation already has with prospects or customers, such as account updates, despatch notices and so on. Or it could be in e-mails which similar but non-competing organisations send.

12 Test, test, test

Finally, turn your attention to how you measure and analyse your campaigns. As we have seen, one of the great strengths of e-mail marketing is that it is so trackable and measurable. Make sure you look closely at what messages, creative approaches, copy, frequency and timing work best for different individuals on your database. Test, test, then test again. Remember – no e-mail marketing campaign is perfect; all you can do is to keep improving.

test, test, then test again

| **Expert interview:** | Ian Hitt, Managing Director, Epsilon International EMEA |

Ian Hitt, MD of e-mail marketing services company Epsilon International EMEA, has worked in direct marketing for 20 years and so can offer a solid understanding not only of how e-mail marketing works but also of how it fits into the overall marketing mix.

AB: Why should readers be interested in e-mail marketing?

IH: E-mail is one of the most effective, measurable and targeted tools at a marketer's disposal. Over the past ten years e-mail marketing has grown hugely, both in volume and in the acceptance of its impact by marketers. In the past couple of years technological advances and a greater focus on analysis and strategy have turned e-mail into an even more sophisticated marketing tool.

With the proliferation of PDAs and handsets such as the iPhone and BlackBerry, we have seen an increase in the use of e-mail. What's more, it's a convenient, non-intrusive form of communication – recipients, whether consumer or business, choose when to open, view and click through, or when to ignore.

AB: It's certainly true that e-mail has been a major marketing tool over the past decade. But where's the evidence that it has a future?

IH: Research shows that e-mail marketing is here to stay. The recent E-mail Marketing Report, published by the Direct Marketing Association, confirms that seven out of ten marketers expect expenditure on e-mail to increase over the next 12 months, despite widespread cuts in marketing budgets. This is backed up by recent Bellwether reports coupled with our engagement with client organisations – we're seeing more of marketing's traditional budget being diverted to e-mail.

Crucially, we're beginning to realise that the benefits of permission-based e-mail marketing campaigns extend far beyond e-commerce transactions and have a significant impact on purchasing behaviour and consumer loyalty in the bricks-and-mortar world. We recently surveyed consumers and found that 50 per cent said they're more likely to buy products from companies that send them e-mail, whether their purchases are online or at a place of business. Upon opening permission-based e-mail, 46 per cent purchase online, 43 per cent purchase offline at retail stores, 29 per cent purchase over the phone, 73 per cent click on a website and 44 per cent watch a video clip. That is a lot of action resulting from, or triggered by, e-mail.

AB: Tell me more about those technological advances – what's new and exciting in e-mail marketing right now?

IH: Video is really taking off. Earlier this year Goodmail Systems launched CertifiedVideo, enabling qualified senders to incorporate rich video and audio content directly into e-mail messaging. The content is automatically triggered when the recipient opens the e-mail to ensure maximum impact.

There has also been a significant rise in retailers sending digital vouchers via e-mail. These allow users to compare prices and offers whilst on the high street. It presents a strong call to action, particularly if timed right as consumers prepare to hit the high street and visit their favourite stores.

Finally, there's been an increased use of e-mail on handheld devices. This is already leading some marketers to optimise their e-mails to be viewed on handsets and the trend is likely to continue. Some retailers are already trialling embedded barcodes in e-mails when they want to incentivise specific products.

AB: What about social media, how is that linking to e-mail?

IH: The integration with social media must be one of the most discussed topics of the past year. E-mails can be social media-enabled, allowing recipients to link the message to their Facebook accounts and share with contacts. It's taking viral marketing a step forward.

AB: What about this enhanced insight and analysis you mentioned?

IH: There has been a significant rise in interest by client organisations in building knowledge around how their e-mail campaigns are working and what their clients are reacting positively to. This creates knowledge and allows marketers to optimise their campaigns for each particular user. The important focus going forward is on effective message targeting and frequency, not on pure volume.

AB: What of the future? What will be coming through in the next year or two?

IH: We will continue to see the growth of Quick Response Codes as a marketing tool linking mobile phone users to a campaign URL. I also think proximity marketing is going to be big. Through GSM localisation, marketers can send timely messages with information or offers to consumers in close proximity of their outlets, or of particular relevance to that location.

At the same time, innovations from ISPs will improve the e-mail experience. Recently, Gmail has developed solutions that allow users to preview documents and avoid sending their messages to the wrong person. Yahoo! has rolled out the new Yahoo! Mail, which includes an increased file size limit (up to 25MB) and drag-and-drop functionality for photos.

Then, of course, there will be further integration with social media and mobile. With social networks and mobile communications becoming more sophisticated and continuing to gather popularity with consumers, e-mail marketers will have to ensure both strategies are aligned, efficient and complementary so that they keep sending the right message at the right time through the right channel.

AB: So, lastly then, what advice would you offer readers on how to run successful e-mail marketing campaigns?

IH: It's essential to ensure quality of your lists, to give people genuine choices on what they receive from you and to always make your content relevant to your recipients. Of course, the success of e-mail hinges heavily on getting subject lines right, too. However, as well as these well-known factors I would advise readers to make considered use of video in their e-mails – it's remarkable just how much can be done with embedded video and the effect it has on response rates.

However, in my view, the most important element of any e-mail marketing campaign is getting the analysis of the results right. The key to successful marketing is understanding what works and what doesn't work, so if you're not constantly analysing and gaining knowledge about what your clients think about your brand then there's a fundamental flaw in your strategy.

Measurement, analysis, insight, knowledge and best practice are key elements of a successful e-mail marketing strategy. We now have the technology to input new data and learnings into our digital campaigns to optimise these in real time. Get this right and everything else will flow from it.

 example

Icelandair

Icelandair is the national carrier of Iceland and its fleet of 12 aircraft make 162 flights a week to 25 destinations, providing not only a convenient stopping-off point for travellers between Europe and North America but also supporting the country's thriving tourist trade. The company has 1,100 employees, one of whom is Katrina Erna Gunnarsdottir, the Marketing Manager.

In her time at the company, Gunnarsdottir has led a complete overhaul of its marketing operations, beginning in 2006 with a rebranding campaign. This introduced a new, lighter look to the company's logo and to the exteriors of its aircraft. Two years later this was carried through to the interiors of the aircraft, the company's uniforms and a revamped website.

Alongside this extensive rebranding, Icelandair introduced an email marketing campaign. Gunnarsdottir explains why: 'We wanted to be closer to our customers, and providing them with useful information by e-mail seemed a targeted, direct and effective way of doing this. It also promised to give us a great way of building loyalty with our guests, creating a buzz around our products, and so driving repeat purchases.'

The company brought on board e-mail marketing specialists ExactTarget, who worked with them to devise and deliver six e-mail campaigns, ranging from newsletters and frequent-flyer updates to pre-flight information messages and post-flight surveys. For example, pre-flight e-mails are sent automatically one week before the flight. They are personalised and give information on check-in, on-board services and the customer's destination. Similarly, post-flight e-mails are automatically sent three days after travel on behalf of Icelandair's CEO. These thank travellers for their custom and ask for feedback via a survey.

The results of this activity have been impressive. In one nine-week period in 2009 the airline's website received 200,000 visits as a result of an e-mail marketing push. That represented a 113 per cent increase in site visits compared with the same period in 2008. These visitors each viewed 5.6 pages and spent 7 minutes and 33 seconds on the site. Consequently, the site booking rate rose from 0.34 per cent to 0.97 per cent, meaning that the airline's bookings increased by 160 per cent between 2008 and 2009.

However, it has not all been plain sailing – or flying even. The campaign needed to reach people across a wide range of countries and so language and time differences were problems that needed to be overcome. Gunnarsdottir explains how she did this: 'Ensuring that every newsletter was properly translated into different languages involved a great deal of work and some useful assistance from ExactTarget's international sending technology. Crucially, this ensured that the coding was in the right language so the e-mails displayed correctly across different countries.

'We also had to deal with different time zones. Timing is central to a campaign like this and it was easy for customers to miss e-mails that arrived in the middle of the night. So we set up a rigorous schedule to ensure every single e-mail was delivered at exactly the right moment.'

Looking to the future, Icelandair plans to further boost e-mail personalisation by integrating data from its web analytics provider, Google Analytics, into ExactTarget. This will allow it to deliver e-mails based on individuals' browsing habits on Icelandair.com. The company also plans to integrate its existing social media strategy into its e-mail efforts, allowing customers to share e-mail content with up to 50 social network sites, including Twitter and Facebook.

Gunnarsdottir has three pieces of advice for any marketer looking to emulate her success with e-mail marketing. 'Firstly,' she says, 'remember that e-mail is largely a matter of discovering what your customers want through trial and error, but that doesn't mean you shouldn't have a strategy. Begin by knowing exactly what it is you want to achieve. Secondly, don't underestimate the power of surveys. We've learned a huge amount about our customers simply by asking them questions, and this has enabled us to personalise our campaigns to good effect. Finally, don't rely too heavily on personalisation – strong creative ideas and execution are always essential in any e-mail marketing campaign.'

 **brilliant** recap

1 On average, in 2009 every $1 spent on e-mail marketing produced a return of $43.62.

2 It is affordable, you can personalise messages and you can closely track performance.

3 While it can be an extraordinarily effective marketing channel, it must be done correctly.

4 You must have clean, accurate data and comply with data protection legislation.

5 Deliver content that appeals and send it at the time when recipients are most likely to read it.

6 Try to encourage a two-way conversation.

7 Closely monitor your delivery rates, open rates and click-through rates.

CHAPTER 7

Blogging

'Be who you are and say what you feel
because those who mind don't matter
and those who matter don't mind.'

Dr Seuss

What we'll cover in this chapter

Not everyone is convinced that blogging can produce business benefits, but more and more are discovering that it can do exactly that. In this chapter you will find:

- the example of London hotel Wyndham Grand Chelsea, which began blogging and within six months had 1,500 visitors a month, around 300 of whom went on to the hotel's main site;
- ten good reasons why you should blog;
- advice on how to decide whether or not blogging is right for you;
- the story of Flourish, a Surrey-based direct marketing agency, which used blogging to grow its turnover to £40,000 a month;
- thoughts on what you should write about in your blog, how to produce a successful blog and how to promote it;
- an interview with Paul Fabretti, who runs blogs for companies such as Dyson and Lexus;
- an insight into how personal stylist iStylista has increased the number of visitors to its website through blogging.

There are now more than 100 million blogs circulating on the Internet. Initially they tended to be individuals holding forth – often ranting – about personal hobbies and passions to a niche audience. Some of the better ones – often those run by former journalists – became very popular. Many of them have hundreds of thousands of subscribers, make large amounts of money from advertisers and are as influential as traditional newspapers and magazines.

More recently, marketers have begun to discover the potential of this new medium and we are witnessing the rise of the company blog. It is not right for every company, but for those who have something to say, who say it well and who can persuade people to read what they have to say, it is in a great many cases proving a useful marketing tool.

 **example**

Wyndham Grand Chelsea

Situated on the Chelsea Harbour, the Wyndham Grand Chelsea is part of a global chain of five-star hotels. It was refurbished in 2009 with a £20 million spend on the introduction of a ballroom, spa and conference facilities.

For hotel marketers, the Internet is increasingly important as more and more potential customers research their hotel options online. Astrid Heitz, Sales Director, says: 'We needed a way of letting those prospects know about our hotel without spending a fortune on search optimisation or search advertising. We'd read about how important content is in pushing you up the rankings and about how it's possible to use specific keywords to generate the right sort of traffic. So in mid-2009 we began to blog. We saw it as a tool that would lead prospects to our site and so ultimately increase bookings.'

The team started slowly and cautiously. They produced a detailed 12-month content strategy which described the topics and keywords they were targeting, then they began producing that content – just 4–6 pieces a month initially. They launched the blog on a sub-domain, using a Wordpress platform.

The results were sudden and startlingly impressive. Within just two months the blog was attracting more than 500 visitors, some of whom were then clicking through to the core website. In just over six months the blog was receiving more than 1,500 visitors a month and this number was growing at 10 per cent a month. Around 300 of those visitors were clicking through to the main website and this led to an increase in bookings.

Heitz describes the blogging campaign as a relatively straightforward exercise. She says: 'It can be a challenge to keep abreast of what's happening in Chelsea and our surrounds because there are so many resources of information to tap. We have to manage our time on it very carefully. But other than that it's been surprisingly straightforward.'

The Wyndham is planning to increase the amount of content it submits to the blog and is integrating other elements of social media. Heitz expects that doing this will further increase traffic to the site and that in the future blogging will generate more visitors than any other means of online marketing. 'Keyword advertising is a waste of time and money,' she says. 'Get blogging right and it not only pays for itself within six months, but you also realise the benefits for years to come with constant traffic trickling through and valuable in-bound links pointing at your site.'

She offers this advice on how to succeed with blogging: 'When planning, get to know the local environment and other related businesses, and connect with them. Write about them and they will do the same for you – it's a great way to make friends in your neighbourhood. The rewards are traffic from their sites, in-bound links and someone who's prepared to talk about you to their loyal clients – blogging opens doors.'

She adds: 'Don't feature content just around your hotel or venue. Think laterally. For example, we featured some content around an exhibition in London on Elvis, it was picked up by *TNT* magazine, which ran a feature on it, and this led to a flurry of bookings.'

A weblog is basically a series of posts in reverse chronological order. It can be text, audio or video, and it usually allows readers to interact with content by voting in polls, posting comments, rating posts and so on. For some small companies it is their primary presence on the Internet and so also includes company, product and service information.

So, why are they all so keen? For one thing, the practicalities of blogging are straightforward and incredibly cheap. You can go to a site such as Wordpress.com, Blogger.co.uk or Typepad.com and in a few minutes you can set up a free, fairly professional-looking blog. Of course, if you want one that integrates with your brand and your existing online presence – and most certainly you should – then it will be a little more complex and expensive, but not much.

However, there is much more to recommend blogging than its affordability. Here are ten benefits businesses gain from blogging.

Ten good reasons why you should blog

1 It pushes your site up the search engines

As we saw in Chapter 3 on search engine optimisation, the search engines rank search results based on the quality and relevance of the content they find. By posting frequent, high-quality blogs you will find that you quickly accumulate a large amount of content that is rich in keywords. The search engine spiders love this and as a result you will find your site moving up the rankings.

2 It persistently reminds people of what you're good at

Blogs are a great way for service providers to demonstrate their expertise or for product vendors to describe the particular benefits of their products. They are an unrivalled forum for all marketers to highlight their passion for whatever it is they do. It could be a firm of accountants commenting on the latest changes to tax legislation, or a wine retailer enthusing about new varieties, or a tour operator providing tips on what to do in different destinations. Whatever it is your company does, you can blog about it and repeatedly put yourself in your customers' and potential customers' minds as experts on that subject.

3 It encourages people to debate issues with you

Crucially, blogs are not one-way communication. Unlike your company website, your press releases, or your product brochure, your blog will allow people to respond. If they find a post particularly useful, they will be able to leave

> your blog will allow people to respond

a comment saying as much. If they vehemently disagree with you, they will be able to make their point. However they respond, you will have an opportunity to develop the conversation, get to know them better, establish a relationship and maybe even sell them something.

4 It provides a space for you to project your personality

People buy from people. No one really likes faceless corporate marketing messages or dull product catalogues. That is why so few ads focus on product attributes. They all try to project a brand, a personality, that customers can relate to and buy into. The tone of voice of the blogosphere is resolutely informal. It is accepted – fully expected, in fact – that you will offer a human perspective, take controversial positions, show what is unique and likeable about your company.

5 It can help you get media coverage

Journalists increasingly use blogs as a source of news stories. Post enough quality content and in time one of these journalists will come across you and ask you to provide comment. This could take your message and your company name to a much wider audience.

 **example**

Paul Murricane of Axis Media Group discovered at first hand how blogging can lead to much wider media coverage. His company provides media interview training and it has a blog which it updates every day with controversial, short and punchy articles. In June 2009 Murricane posted an article about the European elections that week. It was picked up by a journalist on Radio 4's 'PM' programme, who gave Murricane three minutes of network airtime to talk about his training services. How much would you have to pay for three minutes of advertising on national radio?

6 It encourages you to stay abreast of developments in your industry

To write well you must read extensively. Keeping up to date with your industry's blogs is an excellent discipline for staying in touch with new developments, shifting opinions and key people.

7 It sharpens your thinking on key issues

Having to regularly and frequently express a position on topics that are important to you forces you to think about those topics and to clarify your thinking on them.

8 It gives you a platform to convey news about your company

How many people really read your press releases? If you're honest, probably not that many. This means that even your key customers can remain unaware of new services you offer. It also means that if you have a problem – say you need to recall a product batch – you have no established platform for communicating your position.

A blog can provide you with exactly this platform. While many people are blind to news conveyed through traditional media, they increasingly seek out authoritative, popular blogs and believe what they read there.

9 It helps you stand out from your competitors

There may be more than 100 million blogs in existence, but very few of them are company blogs and even fewer are *good* company blogs. You can probably count the number of good company blogs in your sector on one hand. Get your blog right and it can provide a valuable point of competitive advantage.

10 It can be fun

Many people find blogging liberating. It is an opportunity to step outside their day-to-day concerns, to think deeply about an important issue and to connect with new people.

Is it for you?

Without a doubt, then, there is much that you can gain from blogging. However, it should be noted that it is not for everyone. It may cost next to nothing to get started, but that does not mean it is free. It is, in fact, only as free as your time. It can absorb much of your time, so before committing a single minute to it you should check that it is indeed for you. The following three questions should help you to decide.

there is much that you can gain from blogging

1 Do your customers and potential customers read blogs? If very few of them do, then it may not be worth the investment of time. You may be better off spending your time finding them on forums, at the end of a phone or at an industry event.

2 Do you have something interesting to say? In essence, blogs provide a platform to convey an in-depth point of view. You communicate your expertise, enthusiasm, product attributes or whatever through an extended series of posts. If, when it comes to it, you have little to say about your goods, your industry or your work, then your blog will be rather dull and you might end up doing more harm than good to your brand.

brilliant example

Don't assume you have nothing to say. Fiona Humberstone, MD of direct mail agency Flourish in Guildford, began blogging in 2006. She just thought she'd try it out and see what happened. She wrote about subjects that she knew about and provided tips that to her seemed obvious, such as making sure you deliver your leaflets to a house at least three times in order to create an impact.

She has been amazed by how well people have responded. At the time of writing, her blog was receiving more than 200 visitors a day, 70 per cent of her new business meetings were with people who contacted her having read her blog, and 65 per cent of them went on to become clients. Largely as a result of blogging simply about what she knows, she has increased her company turnover to £40,000 per month.

3 Can you commit the necessary time or budget? To build an audience you must post regularly and frequently. There is a good reason television programmes are scheduled for the same time slot every day or every week, and you need to introduce the same reliability into your blogging. If you simply lack the time to do that, you can always hire a ghostwriter to produce it for you. However, if you fail to commit either the time or the budget, your blogging will fail.

What should you blog about?

Once you have decided that blogging is for you and you have set up your blog, the first obstacle that you are likely to encounter is one that stops a great many people – what exactly will you write about?

Coming up with a general theme is relatively easy: you will write about your products, services, sector, work, something that is going to interest your readers and enable you to convey your marketing messages. However, coming up with a topic every day, even every week, can still be tough.

There are three techniques you can use to unlock the content that is inside you. First, ask yourself these questions:

- Who are your readers? Why will they read your blog? What are they looking to get from it? What do they want to read?
- What do you know about? Make a list of all your areas of expertise.
- What do you care about? If everyone agrees with your blog posts, then you should question why you're writing it. Be prepared to be controversial – take a position.

Second, consider the types of blog posts others tend to write:

- Top tips on how to do something well – this can be extended over a lengthy series.
- A 'how to' article that demonstrates your expertise.
- Comment on something in the national news – think how the news of the day links to your business.
- Comment on an industry issue – take a position and generate a debate.
- An insight into the work you do as a company or as an individual – what have you done in the past week that your readers may find interesting?

Finally, look at other blogs in your industry. See what others are writing about. The chances are that will spark some ideas.

Producing your blog

While no one is expecting your blog to be a literary masterpiece, few readers will linger over a blog that has clearly been knocked out in a few minutes without care or attention. Set aside time to write your blog and once you have a first draft, go back over it, editing out these Seven Deadly Sins of Copywriting:

1 Spelling mistakes: use spellcheck, but never rely on it – check it your-self, print it out and check it again, ask someone else to check it for you.

2 Grammar and punctuation errors: buy a good grammar guide, keep it on your desk and refer to it often.

3 Factual inaccuracies: ensure you are accurate with the spelling of people's names and job titles, make sure your numbers add up and always tell the truth!

4 Long sentences: shorter sentences are easier to read and give text greater impact.

5 Overly complex words: always use the simplest, clearest, most direct word available.

6 Unnecessary words: check that every section, paragraph, sentence, phrase, word contributes to your meaning – if it doesn't, cut it.

7 Jargon: avoid industry-specific or technical terms and always be on your guard against business-speak.

By eliminating those seven errors from your writing you will have a post that is better written than the overwhelming majority of blog posts. Take it to the next level by incorporating these blogging-specific writing tips:

● Keep it simple: limit yourself to one simple idea in each post.

● Break it into paragraphs: a larger number of shorter paragraphs are easier to read quickly on a screen.

● Make liberal use of bullet points and lists: again, these help the reader to scan your copy, extracting what is relevant to them.

● Embed links: the Internet is not flat, so make it easy for your readers to gather supporting evidence and read information that may be interesting but is not necessarily directly relevant to the post you are writing.

- Be yourself: remember, blogging is all about authenticity.
- Write something…no matter how short!

All of these tips apply equally if you choose to podcast, webcast or videoblog. All are simple to do and all can make your site more interesting to visitors. Just as no one expects your written blog to be a literary masterpiece, so you are not expected to be a professional presenter. You are, though, expected to look competent and the best way to achieve this is to use the tips above to write a good script, ensure you get good quality recording equipment and then practise your delivery over and over.

Promoting your blog

Most online blogging software allows you to tag your posts so that people can find them using search engines. However, this will produce a limited amount of traffic and you will need to put in some work to promote your blog.

Begin by putting the address of your blog on all your company marketing material: on business cards, on your website, in your email signature, in your brochure and so on. Then start telling people about it. E-mail links to clients, suppliers, friends, contacts. Get in the habit of mentioning it in conversations. Ask people whether they will go there, read what you have written and post comments.

Spend time reading other people's blogs and commenting on them, including a link to your blog. They will probably return the favour and, of course, everyone who reads their blog will see the link to your site. In the next chapter we will see how you can use social media such as Twitter, LinkedIn and Facebook to promote your blog.

Above all else, continue to produce high-quality blogs on a regular and frequent basis. This is what will keep people coming back for more. This is what will encourage them to tell their contacts about your blog. This is what will build a readership for your blog.

Expert interview:	Paul Fabretti, Managing Director, Gabba

Paul Fabretti began blogging in 2005 when he was running a small bathroom business. He found it difficult to persuade people to pay up to £2,000 to a company they had never heard of. For an investment like that they wanted to deal with someone they knew and trusted, which was all very well for the established brands with multi-million-pound marketing budgets, but not so good for Fabretti. He had heard that blogging could be a great way to establish credibility, so he began looking into it more closely.

It proved a great success in promoting that business and from there his interest snowballed. His blogs have been included on the British Interactive Marketing Association's 'Best Blog' shortlist and AdAge's list of the top 150 blogs on social media. In 2009 he set up blogging agency Gabba and within a year he was working with companies such as Dyson and Lexus, helping them to achieve their marketing objectives through blogging.

AB: What exactly does a social media agency do for its clients?

PF: We help businesses with every aspect of their blogging activity, from devising the strategy to setting up the system and even producing the content.

AB: You're clearly passionate about blogging. Why do you think marketers should be considering it?

PF: Well, apart from the way it can help you build credibility, it is also a great way to push your site up the search engine rankings. More than that, though, the proliferation of the Internet means that everyone now has a voice and can comment on your company, so you can't afford not to be in that conversation. You have to be out there, listening to what people are saying about you, engaging with your critics. Customer service is the new marketing.

AB: Is it right for everyone?

PF: No. You should never automatically assume that a blog is the right thing to do. It could be that 90 per cent of the conversation around your brand is taking place in forums, in which case that's where you should focus your energies.

AB: So, how should someone get started?

PF: Always begin with reading. Look at blogs your competitors are writing. Get a feel for the topics they write about, the tone they use. Then work out how you can contribute something relevant, authentic and useful.

AB: What is the greatest mistake people make with blogging?

PF: Dishonesty. In the blogosphere, if you're not authentic you'll soon be found out.

AB: Is it only online businesses that use blogs? Or are we seeing traditional businesses use it as well?

PF: We are seeing more and more businesses adopt blogs. Look at a web start-up these days and there is always a blog attached to this. Perhaps this is simply because they are tech people, but the blog permits the business owners to get across their expertise, the product roadmap and the fixes they intend to implement – it reveals the underbelly of the business. Even 'normal' businesses are beginning to use blogs for the very same reasons: to allow them to show their expertise and demonstrate what makes them better or different from others. This is something which a static website alone cannot do.

AB: Looking ahead, then, what are the trends we're seeing in blogging?

PF: We are seeing quite a significant debate taking place about where the blog sits in the wider scheme of social media strategy. Not too long ago, many considered that with the massive growth of Twitter, blogging in its original, long form was dead. Quick, short, mobile status updates were the future. This missed the real benefit of blogs, which is that they show the people behind the brand, they provide a way of communicating openly what the business is doing, where it is going, and they provide a way for the customer to become part of that journey.

AB: How should blogging fit in with social media as a whole?

PF: Most agree now that the blog should be at the heart of a social media strategy. It is the only long-form way of communicating to and with customers. Twitter and Facebook are largely short, status-led interactions. So blogs are really the only real way that a business can engage to the extent that the consumer wants and deserves.

AB: What about the sites that people use? Is it still the famous ones such as Wordpress and Blogger, or are there new kids on the block?

PF: People have recently flocked to services like Posterous, which allow people to post to a 'Posterous blog' direct from an e-mail. Originally, the beauty of Posterous was mobility. Users could do everything they could on Twitter but they could also post longer-form content. The beauty of a Posterous blog interface is the cleanliness. It is clear and unfussy.

AB: But do businesses want to provide this sort of running commentary on where they are and what they're doing?

PF: Probably not. In fact, the irony of Posterous is that bloggers have continued to write War And Peace-length posts. To me, that suggests that the long form of blogging remains crucial to the evolution of blogs.

 **example**

iStylista.com

Personal stylist Chantelle Zinderic established iStylista in 2007. Initially it was intended as a channel to sell personalised style guides to women all over the world. It was relaunched in June 2009 offering members their own online changing room where they can see clothing items most suited to their body shape, natural colouring, body niggles, budget, age and so on.

Members pay nothing to sign up. The company makes its money in 10–15 per cent commission on clothing sales, style guide sales and advertising. The site has 20,000 members and recently achieved a place in *The Independent's* list of the top 100 fashion websites.

Blogging has, from the start, been an important way for iStylista to generate traffic, to keep people on the site and to grow the database of members. Zinderic says: 'Building a database is becoming harder as web users become more fickle, so we felt by sharing items of interest and value we'd be more likely to win hearts and minds, encourage registration on the website and ultimately build loyalty.'

At the same time she wanted to push the site up the search engine rankings and saw blogging as a good way of achieving that aim. 'Content is king when it comes to SEO,' she says. 'Google is refining its search algorithms and therefore we needed to adjust accordingly, targeting less competitive, long-tail keywords around female wellbeing, fashion and lifestyle. These all appear in the blog posts and get us high up the rankings for high-conversion, specific searches.'

The team at iStylista devised a 12-month content strategy based on those keywords. By targeting some popular search phrases – such as 'What body shape am I?' – with blog content on that topic, iStylista started moving up the search rankings.

Zinderic reports that the greatest challenge at the outset was finding the time and budget to blog on a regular basis. She says: 'For the first three months we got very little traction, and without the overall strategy to keep us focused and inspired we would have struggled.' The effort has been worthwhile, however. The company receives 30 per cent of its web traffic from the blog and the volume of that traffic increases by roughly 5 per cent every month. The blog has also been responsible for some of the website's thousands of in-bound links, which in turn has improved search positioning dramatically.

Looking ahead, iStylista will soon be adding video content to the blog in order to increase user 'stickiness' to the site and brand. The company has also started working with Southampton Solent University, selecting a number of its best Fashion Stylist third-year students and tasking them with the production of content on an ongoing basis. The work forms part of the students' coursework and is invaluable content for iStylista.

Zinderic offers this advice to anyone beginning to blog: 'Blogging is an integral part of modern marketing, but it needs to be effectively planned for maximum impact. Time management is also incredibly important – it's very easy to waste a few hours a day on this and get very little return for the initial six months, especially if you don't effectively target the right keyphrases in the right manner. Don't take a blog lightly. Plan, plan, plan! Do your research into what else is out there in your market and take the elements you like, but also create something different. Define your writing style, when you are going to write, what you are going to write, and list out your top 100 key phrases to target.

'Share responsibility and get the entire team involved in the exercise of blogging, but don't let the blog draw focus from your core business. As you start getting results, then you can put in more time and effort. Finally, keep evaluating what you are doing and don't just regurgitate things from other sites. Make yours different and ensure it positions you as a thought leader and someone passionate about your field.'

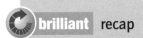 **recap**

1 A blog can be a good way of communicating a relatively complex point to your target audience; it offers more space to put your arguments than you receive in most marketing communications.

2 It will work only if you have something to say, your audience is willing to read it and you execute the plan effectively.

3 Write on topics you care about, write professionally and with passion.

4 Push your blog out through every possible avenue.

5 Read and comment on other blogs and those bloggers will return the compliment.

Social media

'The way of the world is meeting people through other people.'

Robert Kerrigan

What we'll cover in this chapter

There is a great deal of excitement about the potential surrounding social media and indeed it can be a useful marketing tool. However, it is essential to understand it and to approach it correctly. In this chapter you will find:

- the story of how brewer Adnams got started in social media;
- the story of how youth marketing agency Love Communications used social media to convey information about swine flu prevention to 10,000 young people in just three hours;
- details of the main social media platforms;
- advice on how to succeed in social media marketing;
- an interview with Tanya Goodin, Chief Executive of Tamar, one of Media Momentum's top 50 'hottest, fastest-growing digital media companies in the UK';
- the story of how Marmite used social media to launch its latest brand extension.

---

 example

Adnams

Adnams is best known as a brewer. The Suffolk-based company owns 70 pubs around the country and at any one time can be supplying beer to up to 1,000 other venues, such as hotels and golf clubs. It also produces a range of wines, all of which are in the more expensive £10-plus category, and owns nine Cellar & Kitchen stores and two

▶

hotels. The final part of its portfolio is a pub with rooms in Suffolk – when the previous landlord retired the Adnams hotel team got the opportunity to put their experience of running hotels to use in the pub with bed and breakfast. Adnams is, then, a complex company, with 400 employees and a wide range of activities.

Sean Clark, Head of Web, began using social media in 2008. 'Our customers had set up an Adnams appreciation society on Facebook,' he recalls. 'So we'd input to that on an ad hoc basis where and when it was relevant. I'd set up a Twitter account and a Facebook profile and had tried getting people to visit it. We weren't doing anything serious – we were just playing around with this new channel.'

However, it got him thinking and he decided there was an opportunity to build the wine side of the business through this channel. 'Selling wine online is a very competitive business,' he explains. 'We can't compete with the prices or the online spend that some of our competitors offer. We'd found it really tough to get traction through e-mail, banner ads or search. There's no point being found on "red wine" because people searching for that almost always want cheap deals. It's possible to bid on specific region names and we'd had some success doing that, but it's incredibly time-consuming. You can't outsource it because the person doing the bidding needs to know their wines and it's pretty rare that you find a wine expert who also understands search.'

So Adnams was looking for a new way to market its wines. Clark realised that social media was the ideal channel. 'It struck me that Twitter in particular would allow us to find people who were talking about our brands, to answer their questions and so build relationships.' Like many people starting out in social media, he quickly found that it confounded his expectations. 'Very quickly I discovered that there was potential in social media for us to market our products, but that it wasn't wine people were talking about – it was beer.'

Many people become disillusioned with social media when they find it fails to conform to their initial expectations. Clark did not fall into this trap. 'I decided early on not to fight it. I wouldn't arrive at a party and immediately insist that everyone there start talking about what I wanted to talk about. If people were asking me about beer, then I'd talk about beer.'

This flexible approach has yielded results for Adnams. The company has 1,400 followers on Twitter and has engaged many loyal customers in conversations that not only strengthen those ties to all-important customers but also give the company's employees valuable feedback. 'Our master brewer can now talk directly to the person drinking it,' says Clark.

It is still early days and Clark has yet to specify objectives for his social media engagement. He says that people have bought products they have seen discussed on Twitter or on the new Facebook pages that the nine store managers are setting up. However, at this stage it is less about generating sales and more about brand representation. Clark says: 'The conversation is already happening in social media. People are out there talking about Adnams, so it's important that we join in.'

He offers this advice: 'No marketers can afford to ignore this channel. At the very least you need to look at the various social media and find out what, if anything, people are saying about your brand. Once you've done that you can decide how best to interact. Twitter may not be right for you; it may be that your customers are on LinkedIn or Bebo. Find out where they are and start talking with them. You may be surprised where it leads you.'

Social media has, without doubt, been the online phenomenon of the past few years. Its growth has been meteoric. In August 2008 Facebook had 100 million users; by February 2010, it had reached 500 million users. At that rate of growth, by 2011 it would have 630 million users. It has a larger population than any country other than China or India.

While Facebook remains the most popular online social networking site, it is by no means the only one. Early in 2010 Twitter announced that it had reached the benchmark of 50 million tweets sent every day. Then there is YouTube, Bebo, MySpace, Club Penguin and so on, not to mention all the business networks such as LinkedIn, Ecademy and Viadeo.

In the UK at the start of 2010 more than 10 per cent of all Internet visits were to these social media sites, compared with 12 per cent to search engines and 12 per cent to entertainment sites. In 2009, social media really entered the mainstream: the Prime Minister, Gordon Brown, famously addressed the nation through YouTube, while the Christmas number one came about as a result of a Facebook campaign.

It is not only the numbers of people using these sites that is growing – just as importantly, the amount of time they spend on them is growing. A report from Nielsen Research revealed that across the globe, average time spent on social networking sites grew from just over two hours per month in December 2007 to just over five and a half hours in December 2009.

'The Internet is a giant international network of intelligent, informed computer enthusiasts, by which I mean, "people without lives". We don't care. We have each other.'

Dave Barry

With so many people spending so much time on these sites it is no wonder that so many marketers are interested. More than any other channel there is the possibility on social media for your campaign to go viral and thus reach millions of people.

brilliant example

Many marketers wrongly believe that social media marketing is relevant only when aimed at a young audience. While they are wrong – more than 50 per cent of social media users are aged over 35 – social media is undoubtedly a good place to find and connect with that hard-to-influence youth audience – 15–21 year olds now spend four and a half hours a day online, predominantly on social networking sites.

When youth marketing agency Love Communications set up an e-team in 2009 it launched its Swine Flu Skank campaign to show just how effective a medium it can be. It took a message that was high on the news agenda and repackaged it to make it relevant for the youth audience. It teamed the NHS's 'Catch it, Bin it, Kill it' tag line with the Skank dance craze that was spreading across the UK club scene and created the Swine Flu Skank, a catchy, credible and amusing song promoting a real message.

It launched the video on a Friday evening when social networking traffic in this age group is at its peak. The e-team housed the video on YouTube and then seeded the link on Facebook. Regional reps seeded it into their own networks to quickly take the message across the UK. Meanwhile, the video was sent directly to leading opinion formers, including Radio 1 and 1Xtra, MTV and club DJs. The 'top and bottom' approach quickly caused an online phenomenon and spread through to Bebo, MySpace and online forums.

Within 3 hours, the Swine Flu Skank had been viewed 10,000 times. Within 24 hours, the video was the number one most discussed, most viewed, most favourited and most rated video in the UK, and the no. 10 rated music video on YouTube globally – 85 per cent of the 2,000 public comments on YouTube were positive, with quotes from the UK, Europe, Japan, India, the US and Canada. Within 24 hours, the video had been reposted from YouTube onto 20,000 Bebo profiles and 30,000 Facebook profiles. There are currently around 40 different versions of the Swine Flu Skank on YouTube, many featuring young people recreating the dance or creating new videos in their own style.

E-mails have come in from young people asking for performances in their schools, and both Leeds HMPS and NHS Camden have requested the video to use in their prisons and surgeries. The song was played on Radio 1 (Chris Moyles' Breakfast Show, Tim Westwood Rap Show), BBC 1Xtra (Ace & Vis on Drivetime), Choice FM (Breakfast Show) and numerous specialist and community radio stations, including Ministry of Sound Radio, Diesel:U: Music, Ujima (Bristol) and Aston FM (Birmingham).

Sam Brown, MD at Love Communications, says: 'The campaign worked because it was created by young people and so they felt they owned it. Overall, the message is presented in a humorous way without disparaging the seriousness of the issue. Not only has this shown the potential of social media as a marketing platform but there is now a huge opportunity to use the swine Flu Skank to communicate the NHS's message to young people to help prevent the further spread of swine flu within this audience.'

However, there is much more to social media marketing than viral campaigns and it would be a mistake to base your strategy in this area on the possibility of developing one. In truth, they are few and far between and they tend to work only by accident. Deliberately creating one can reek of inauthenticity and, as we will see, that is the death knell for any social media campaign.

Instead, social media is a great place to gradually build a community of people with whom you interact. It allows you to target your activity. You can identify a specific niche – say, music fans on Spotify, celebrity spotters on Zimbio or slideshow sharers on SlideShare – and talk with them about that specific subject.

It also allows you to reach people at a point of high engagement. Advertising around sporting occasions has always attracted a premium because people care about sport and about the team they are watching, and advertising around it allows a brand to tap into that passion. The same is somewhat true of social media. People are there to discuss an interest or connect with friends and so tend to be highly engaged and receptive. They've chosen to be there – you're not having to intrude on them.

Perhaps best of all, though, social media is free to use. This is revolutionising the world of marketing. Where in the past a small company had no chance of competing with a multinational competitor with a multi-million-pound budget and access to all the most desirable marketing channels, now the playing field is considerably more level. True, the multinational can spend millions on creative, but in terms of the media space itself, both companies have exactly the same access.

The only cost of social media marketing is the time it takes to do it. This should not be underestimated, however. It is a highly addictive activity and many novices find that it can consume hours, days, weeks even, then produce little real return.

 'Give a person a fish and you feed them for a day; teach that person to use the Internet and they won't bother you for weeks.'

Anonymous

It is essential, therefore, to understand the options, to lay out your objectives clearly and to devise a plan that will achieve those objectives. In the rest of this chapter we will look at exactly how to do that.

The main social media platforms

There will be many platforms that are specific to your industry. For example, in the digital media and marketing industry there is e-consultancy, NMA Register and the Interactive Advertising Bureau. They all operate their own social media platforms and anyone working in the digital media and marketing industry should use them.

However, there are also many platforms that could be relevant to every marketer. If you've never looked at any of these, log on now and start exploring. You may find that a surprising number of your potential customers are there. You may find a new channel to market, one that those prospects have chosen to visit and where they're discussing something they care about, and one that is free to access.

What are you waiting for?

1 Facebook

With 500 million users, Facebook has enormous potential for any marketer. It also holds an unprecedented amount of information about those users' lives. It knows what they do, what they like, who they know and so on – you can use this information to target your ads more effectively.

Facebook has enormous potential for any marketer

It is fairly quick and straightforward to create and post your ads and with Facebook's reporting tools you can closely track your campaign's performance and improve your ad. Also, payment is dependent on results, so it is a low-risk form of advertising.

brilliant example

CM Photographic used Facebook and the data contained in its status updates to target its exact demographic: 24–30-year-old women who are about to get married and so need a wedding photographer. Over 12 months, the company made nearly $40,000 from a $600 advertising investment on Facebook.

2 Twitter

Twitter use has grown exponentially. Between February 2008 and February 2009 it grew by 1,382 per cent. Marketers use it to tell followers about special offers or deals, about product launches and company news. Others use it simply for customer service by tracking what people are saying about their company and sending dissatisfied customers a direct message to resolve their problem. It is also useful for building a buzz around an event, a blog or, more generally, a brand.

In April 2010 Twitter began tentatively to allow advertising, or what it called Promoted Tweets. It was a low-key, cautious introduction, but may signal greater opportunities for advertisers further down the line.

3 YouTube

Hard though it may be to believe, YouTube was founded only in 2005. In such a short space of time it has become an integral part of many people's lives. In fact, every minute 24 hours of footage is uploaded to YouTube.

Marketers have used YouTube to run video advertising, such as InVideo Ads or YouTube video ads, to sponsor contests, to create brand channels and, of course, to add their own content to the site. Through YouTube Insight they can view detailed statistics about the videos that they upload to the site.

4 LinkedIn

LinkedIn is a business network. Members enter their career and education details and link to their business contacts. They then link to the contacts of their contacts and so on. Users can recommend their contacts, ask for specific introductions and comment in forums.

By 2010 it had more than 75 million members in more than 200 countries and it is growing fast. A new member joins LinkedIn approximately every second. Executives from all Fortune 500 companies are LinkedIn members.

Marketers use it very much as they do offline business networking. If you sell to businesses it can be a great place to find customers and promote your products or services. Regardless of whether you sell to businesses or customers, it can be useful for making contacts of all sorts.

5 Viadeo

Viadeo is a competitor to LinkedIn. By 2010 it had 30 million users worldwide and around 120,000 unique visitors a month (www.viadeo. com), so it is smaller than LinkedIn. However, it is growing fast and it offers a range of apps that allow you to do things such as integrate polls, import presentations and share video through your profile.

6 Ecademy

Founded in 1998, Ecademy is one of the oldest online social networks. It promises a community of businesspeople sharing knowledge, building their networks and growing their businesses.

Principles of success in social media

No matter which platform you choose, there are several golden rules that apply across all social media marketing. It is important to be aware of these and to follow them closely. Social media marketing is quite unlike more traditional marketing and, because it is all about building reputation and creating a brand that people want to connect with, naïve mistakes can be fatal.

Take time to plan your strategy, implement it carefully and, above all else, learn the lessons of those who have done it already. The following six steps should ensure you don't go too far wrong.

1 Watch, listen and learn

Before you dive in, spend some time observing the platform or platforms where you want to build a presence. You can join almost every online social network without charge and once you have done that you can quietly watch, listen and learn.

Think of it like visiting a party and rather than striding confidently to the middle of a room, introducing yourself and starting to recount your favourite anecdote, spending a little time acclimatising yourself, getting a feel for the atmosphere, listening to what others are talking about, seeing who is there and how they are behaving.

2 Give it a go

Once you have a basic feel for how the platform operates it is time to give it a go. Just as you don't want to be the brash outsider at the party who makes an immediate spectacle of himself, equally you don't want to be the silent wallflower who never speaks to anyone.

Start building a profile. Connect with a few people you know already and a few you don't. Play around with the technology and discover what is possible. Familiarise yourself with how it all works and start to get a feel for how others are using it as a marketing channel.

3 Devise objectives and a plan

By now you should have an initial idea of what you might be able to achieve through engagement with this social media. Before you do anything else, make a plan. Identify some specific objectives, targets you want to reach, and a plan for how you will do that.

Social media can be extremely addictive and remarkably time-consuming. Without a clear plan you can quickly find you have spent hours and hours just building a network, interacting with interesting people or perfecting your profile, and while it has all been great fun, you haven't done anything to promote your company.

4 Have a message that interests people

Begin with clarity about the message you want to convey on social media. You know by now the type of subjects people discuss on your social media platform. You know what interests them. So decide what aspects of your product or your service will interest those people. Then think about the language or the visuals you want to use and how they will fit in with other content on the site.

5 Converse, don't sell

Social media is not like advertising or, say, direct marketing, where you can simply fire marketing messages at people and wait for a percentage of them to respond. It is more subtle than that. People expect to have genuine conversations. Use marketing-speak and they will quickly stop listening to you. Think about where you can add genuine value to the people on this platform.

Think of it like networking in the real world. If you turn up to an event and start giving everyone the hard sell on your product or company, pretty soon you'll find yourself standing alone next to the canapés. Successful networkers turn up hoping to meet interesting new people, to find out about what they do and to make a connection for the future. It's less about what they can do for you in the short term and more about who they know who might prove a valuable contact in the long term. Precisely the same principle applies to online networking.

6 Start small and be consistent

Too many marketers have rushed into social media, believing all the hype and expecting it to be an immediate road to untold riches. Of course, it isn't. However, that doesn't mean it is an empty shell, no more than media hype. It is perfectly possible to use social media as an effective tool, it just takes careful and consistent application over a sustained period of time.

> it is perfectly possible to use social media as an effective tool

Begin small. Allocate a limited amount of time or resource to the project, have clearly defined objectives and a carefully considered plan. Do not expect to see immediate results. Be prepared to wait several months. Review progress regularly. If it isn't working, change the plan. If it is working, then start to invest more heavily in it.

Expert interview: Tanya Goodin, Chief Executive Officer, Tamar

Tamar is one of the UK's leading search and social media digital agencies. Under Goodin's leadership over the past 15 years, the company has grown significantly and now has more than 30 major clients over three continents within the financial services, retail and travel industries.

Goodin was a finalist in the 2007 Ernst & Young Entrepreneur of the Year awards and the 2008 BlackBerry Outstanding Women and Technology awards. In 2009 Tamar was voted Agency of the Year by Financial Services Forum members.

▶

It is one of Media Momentum's top 50 'hottest, fastest-growing digital media companies in the UK'.

AB: There's been a lot of hype around social media. Is it justified?

TG: Absolutely! It's almost universally agreed that social media is going to be the fastest-growing communications channel over the next few years.

AB: But just because everyone's talking about it doesn't mean it's actually important. Isn't it all just hype?

TG: No. Let me give you a few facts abut social media. At the start of 2009, Twitter usage was growing at 1,382 per cent year-on-year. According to Nielsen Online, in January 2009 alone, US usage doubled in a single month.

In 38 years there will be 50 million radio listeners in the world. Television will reach that number in just 13 years, but the Internet will achieve it in only four, and the iPod in three. However, Facebook added 100 million users in less than nine months. Facebook now has 500 million active users worldwide, with the fastest-growing demographic being over-55 women.

More than 20 hours of video content are uploaded to YouTube every single minute. It is the second largest search engine in the world. 25 per cent of search results for the World's Top 20 largest brands are links to user-generated content.

AB: OK, so social media is popular. But still, what does this mean for business? Have any companies actually made any money out of it all?

TG: Yes. Dell claims to have made over $3 million via its Twitter activities alone. Sony used a Facebook widget to drive approximately 11 million visits to a contest page around the film 30 Days of Night. Adidas leveraged mobile social media to increase retail revenues in Las Vegas on the NBA All Star game by a multiple of 20.

AB: So, how does it work?

TG: Social media marketing is, in essence, about brands connecting with their consumers and potential customers in a language they understand and in the places where they relax online. It's not about expecting consumers to come to you; it's about going to them and listening to what they're saying about you and your competitors. Social media marketing is all about reaching out and connecting with people. It's not about press releases, or talking at people. It's listening to them and solving problems, taking suggestions, utilising ideas, making the most of brand advocates and generally respecting your customers.

AB: But in practical terms, how can my readers actually get involved?

TG: There are so many ways, it's hard to know where to start. You can connect with and respond to consumers on sites like Twitter and Facebook. You can entertain and engage consumers using competitions, games and widgets. You can build brand awareness through social presences, engagement and innovation.

The Greek philosopher Epictetus said that we have two ears and one mouth so that we can listen twice as much as we speak, and the first step in any wise social media marketing campaign is to listen. Until you know what people are saying or not saying about you, making a strategy of engagement is pointless.

You don't have to invest thousands in expensive monitoring services. You can gain a lot of insight by using free sites like Technorati, Google Alerts, SocialSeek and just plain old search engines.

AB: What other advice would you offer people on how to use social media as an effective marketing tool?

TG: Don't patronise people. They know when brands are being false and will call you out on it. Talk in the same language as the people you are hoping to engage with. Have a long-term plan – don't jump in with a bang and then let things tail off to nothing, and don't start off your marketing without a comprehensive plan of attack.

AB: What about measuring success? How do you know if something's working?

TG: The key is to take as many measurements as possible. That way you'll be able to spot uplifts more easily. Look at the number of interactions with your page, the number of fans or followers you're getting, number of subscribers, and all the classic on-site analytics like time spent on pages, referrals, registrations, bounce rates and so on.

AB: What of the future? What will be coming through in the next year or two?

TG: There will be many more linkages between different technologies and social media platforms, for example GPS, location-based, real-time information giving you a clearer picture of where your contacts and friends are and what they're doing.

 **example**

Marmite

'Marmite is a product that people either love or hate,' admits Tom Denyard, Marketing Manager: Marmite for Unilever UK and Ireland. 'We never try to pretend everyone loves it. We try to be honest in everything we do.' This is a brand strategy that appears to be working: Marmite has a retail sales value of £50 million, £40 million of which comes from the core spread and £10 million from the spin-off crisps, rice cakes and breadsticks.

Perhaps because of its quirky appeal, Marmite has always had a strong social media following. A Facebook page was created by fans and grew organically because of their interest. Unilever is now involved in running it, but ownership is collective. Everyone on the page has a stake, everyone has an equal voice. There are more than 400,000 fans on Facebook as well as bloggers and regular tweeters supporting the brand.

So when the Marmite team had a new product extension, Marmite XO, to launch, they decided to use social media. Denyard says: 'This was a way to give them something back and to engage them not just in the launch but the development and promotion of the product. The creation of the Marmarati is something that they've been able to throw their energy at and we've been able to use to reward them for their devotion.'

The first step was to devise the concept of the Marmarati, a Victorian secret society that had been the guardians of the Marmite brand for a century. The story was that this Marmarati were, with the launch of XO, revealing themselves to the world to mark that centenary and to recruit the next generation of members.

In collaboration with the agency We Are Social, the team identified the 30 people online who had created the most content around the brand and had been most positive about it, and invited them to an event held in a fabulous listed building in central London. The invitation was full of hammed-up Victorian language and intrigue, and it immediately sparked online chatter about what the Marmarati could be, what the event might be for, why the individuals might have been chosen.

When the chosen 30 arrived they found red velvet drapes, sterling silver candelabras, low lighting, dark wood, a luxuriously laid banqueting table and a master of ceremonies to walk the guests through the 'big reveal': why they were there, the importance of their task and the introduction to the members of the Marmarati Inner Sanctum. Guests were initiated into the society with an oath of allegiance, conducted a blind tasting of three versions of XO at the banqueting table and gave their feedback to influence its development.

The event was hosted by the Marmite marketing team, all in period Victorian costumes. Denyard was the Host of the First Circle, the name given to the 30 people who had been invited to the event. The MD of Marmite in the UK played his role as Lord Marmarati, signing their initiation certificates personally. The creative director of the design agency was the Master Artisan, and the research and development expert the Master Alchemist.

Denyard recalls: 'After the "big reveal" we spent the evening with the guests, drinking Marmite-infused cocktails and eating Marmite-inspired canapés. We showed them old manufacturing equipment that we'd brought down from the factory and first draft designs of how Marmite XO could look. Our First Circle loved it and we finally wrapped things up well into the early hours!'

The First Circle left that evening with a lot to talk about and a very specific brief: to recruit people to the Second Circle. This Second Circle had to apply for entry by uploading something to the website that would demonstrate their love for Marmite. They sent everything from poems to films – 846 entries were approved for publication from a total of 1,200 uploads and 25,000 visits to the website in five weeks.

Of these entrants, 160 were selected by a public vote as the winners and they, with the original 30, each received one of only 200 prototype commemorative jars of Marmite XO, beautifully made with a wax-dipped lid and a wax seal on the front with the Marmarati crest in gold. There was also a set of instructions, asking them to conduct a tasting ceremony and film their reactions.

It was a first for everyone involved at Marmite – a genuine break from traditional marketing techniques. Denyard says: 'This has been a learning experience for everyone involved, but I have to say that at every stage it has exceeded our expectations. We were worried a few times. Would people come to the launch event? Would they post entries on the website? But each time these proved to be unfounded and we've had a brilliant response and a huge amount of interest.'

He believes that so far the campaign has reached around 750,000 people. Furthermore, all those involved have chosen to be there. Denyard says: 'For a product like XO, which is aimed at a small band of dedicated fans, that's exactly where we would want to be. And from my point of view, it's fantastic to have a new product going to market based on the feedback of our most hardcore fans. It gives me a lot of confidence that the product will be a success when it hits the shelves.'

The campaign has been such a success that Marmite plans to do more social media work in the future. Denyard says: 'Social media can give people a sense of having been heard and of ownership. It's a vehicle for democratising the brand. With a brand like Marmite, which captures the imagination of its "lovers" in such a unique way, that has to be a good thing, building the brand for the future.'

He offers this advice on how other marketers can emulate the social media success of Marmite: 'Begin by asking whether it is the right thing for your brand. It's very sexy to play around with social media at the moment. Everyone wants to be on Twitter and to have a Facebook page, produce cool content and be cutting edge in this space. The fact is it can't be right for everyone. There's a real danger of being fashionable but playing no role for your consumers. You start with your audience and take it from there. That said, once you're sure you're playing in the right space, throw the kitchen sink at it. If you are going to do it, give as much of yourself to it as possible. At a few points during this campaign, we had to decide how far we should go, and at every point we decided to be as ballsy as possible. For example, we used the marketing team and not actors and we blindfolded the guests for the tasting. It paid off every time in making the experience so much better. So be brave. If you're not, you won't get any cut-through. It's a busy place to play, with lots of cool stuff being created every day – and if your stuff doesn't stand out, it's wasted.'

In conclusion, he says: 'Invest the time and effort up front. Nail a great creative idea before pushing the button on the campaign and do the research to work out who your key influencers are. Then be generous. Reward the people who come on the journey with you. They are good enough to give you their time and to be involved, so make sure you make them feel special.'

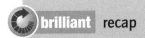 **recap**

1 Millions of people are spending a large proportion of their waking hours on social media sites.

2 Viral campaigns on social media can be phenomenally effective, but you can also use it as a place to build your brand and promote your products.

3 In addition to the well-known sites such as Facebook, Twitter and YouTube, there are many more niche sites where you may be able to network to good effect.

4 Begin by watching, getting a feel for the tone and content of conversations on the site. Only then begin to interact and build your network.

5 Don't try the hard sell on social media sites – it doesn't work.

CHAPTER 9

Online PR

'Some are born great, some achieve greatness, and some hire public relations officers.'

Daniel J. Boorstin

What we'll cover in this chapter

The Internet has transformed PR. In this chapter you'll find:

- insight into the way this has happened;
- advice on how you can use the Internet to create a buzz around your products and services;
- an interview with online PR guru Mark Terry-Lush;
- the story of how online shopping download Invisible Hand used PR to boost awareness of its service.

Public relations used to be relatively straightforward. You worked out which publications your target audience read, then you approached the journalists on those titles and somehow persuaded them to write nice things about you. Sometimes this involved sending well-written press releases. At other times you would pitch original, interesting article ideas to them. Very often it involved taking them out for lunch and getting them familiar and friendly with your key spokespeople.

It was straightforward, but it was effective. A positive write-up in a widely read and respected publication could be worth acres of pages of advertising. Crucially, the readers knew you hadn't paid for the write-up in the same way you had paid for the advertising. The commendation, or the mention, came from an impartial journalist whom they trusted and so was even more powerful than advertising.

That sort of PR work still exists. Walk into any newsagent and you will see shelves full of newspapers and magazines. Many of them are widely read and still greatly respected. While that remains the case, there will always be a place for traditional PR. However, the rise of the Internet has added a whole new dimension to the media and created many new opportunities to gain coverage. The Internet has changed PR in three ways.

the rise of the Internet has added a whole new dimension to the media

First, the Internet is changing how companies reach journalists of all types. E-mailed press releases are now the norm and online services such as Response Source, which help connect journalists and spokespeople, are commonplace, but increasingly companies are using social media tools such as Twitter to contact journalists.

brilliant tip

Try putting 'journalists on Twitter' into a search engine. At the time of writing this produced a list of more than 600 journalists with their Twitter addresses.

Second, traditional print media are no longer the only show in town. Increasingly, people are reading the online versions of those publications, or they are reading online-only publications, or they are reading blogs, or they are interacting with friends and strangers in online forums and on other social media platforms. This means that, just as it is important for companies to manage their reputation on social media – as we have already seen in Chapter 8 – so they need to target key bloggers and online journalists.

Third, companies are changing the way in which they communicate with journalists and bloggers. Where in the past they might have carpet-bombed these key influencers with press releases, increasingly they are taking a more one-to-one approach. The ease of contact increases the number of possible interactions and so the pressure is on to identify the most relevant person and present them with carefully targeted information.

Personalised relations increasingly is becoming the focus for PR. The broad-brush approach that in the past was the tactic of the PR industry is being broken down by increasing pressure from journalists and bloggers for one-to-one communications, where the pitch is personalised and demonstrates a deep understanding of their subject area. Beware, however: there are a number of blacklists out there where marketers and their PR agencies who are continuing to spam bloggers and journalists are being named and shamed. It's down to the client to make sure that their PR agency is undertaking personalised relations on their behalf and appreciating social media ethics. Failure to do this could mean their brand or company bears the brunt of any criticism.

Taken together, these three developments are producing a revolution in the way companies seek to generate a buzz. Increasingly, they are appointing PR and social media managers in recognition of the fact that the two are intertwined. It's all about creating a buzz, regardless of whether you do it directly through your blog or social media engagement, or via a medium such as a journalist or blogger.

Expert interview: **Mark Terry-Lush, Founder and Director, Renegade Media**

Mark Terry-Lush describes himself as a specialist in the convergence of public relations and social media. As the founder and Director of PR and digital marketing agency Renegade Media, he has been involved in the creation and management of global online communities, through to blogger outreach, brand management and content distribution. Over the years he has run online PR campaigns for MINI, Converse, ASICS, Onitsuka Tiger, Under Armour, K-Swiss, Courvoisier and a number of B2B brands.

AB: Why is online PR better than traditional PR?

MT-L: It's not necessarily. We used to be a traditional PR agency, but we discovered that by fusing our traditional skills with the new digital channels we could produce better results for our clients. The change happened very quickly, but we had to react to shifting client demands.

The results can be stunning, but we never try to persuade clients to use online channels if they're not suitable. We hand-hold their senior teams and help them understand the pros and cons of digital.

▶

AB: Why should they be interested in this?

MT-L: The world has changed. The post-recession marketing landscape is digital. Conversations are online. 94 per cent of executives report that they are using Web 2.0 technologies to change the way their companies communicate on an internal framework.

Cloud applications and social networks change the way we hire, monitor, commute and collaborate as people within a community of purpose. As brand owners, 87 per cent of companies are using the new social framework to reach out to customers, whether that is through digital campaigns or customer relations channels.

AB: What does online PR, or PR 2.0 as you put it, actually involve?

MT-L: We train our clients on how to use social media. We monitor and manage their online reputations. We run blogger and consumer outreach campaigns. We use online channels to communicate with and influence journalists.

AB: Tell me more about blogger outreach. What does that mean and why should marketers be interested in it?

MT-L: Blogger outreach is perhaps the most controversial and unique service that Renegade offers. Firstly, it involves creating websites that act as hubs for blog content that is relevant to the campaign we're running. Secondly, it involves building relationships with some of the most powerful and influential bloggers across all sectors.

AB: How do you do that?

MT-L: We introduce them to brands through sponsored events, broadcasts and support programmes. The key to ensuring the right content is published by the most influential people is to provide information in a new informal structure, free from the constraints and commercial styling of traditional public relations.

AB: Why do it?

MT-L: Get it right and your company or product can often feature on a blog that has more readers than a daily newspaper, but also has the credibility of an organic reaction. Deep-level investigation will find that the stories hitting the headlines in traditional media are often driven by a select few whose opinions filter through the Web.

AB: What do you mean by organic reaction?

MT-L: People perceive blogs as the little guys, free from editorial control and so less partial than the traditional media. That makes it much more credible when they endorse or even mention a brand.

AB: Are they genuinely that impartial?

MT-L: For the most part, yes. Some blogs have become 'super-blogs'. They are so famous that they become over-commercialised. They can still be valid opinion-formers, but very often it is the little guys who have the most influence.

AB: How can my readers begin to influence these bloggers?

MT-L: The only way to begin a successful relationship with a blogger is to locate one who truly echoes your own beliefs. Beneficial relationships can only flourish if you absolutely respect each other. Your readers should remember that in the blogosphere they'll be having conversations they might not necessarily have in their everyday lives, so make absolutely certain you know what you're talking about and that you are comfortable talking about it before venturing into the world of blogger relations.

AB: What are the secrets to doing it successfully?

MT-L: The best advice I can give is to maintain personal relationships with a small number of blogs, forums and communities. There is no secret to successful relationships, so trust your instincts and be yourself. Divulge your interests and offer an open channel of communication rather than a push of information. Take them for a beer.

 **example**

Invisible Hand

Invisible Hand is an add-on to browsers such as Mozilla Firefox, Microsoft Internet Explorer and Google Chrome. It shows alternative prices of products that users search for on those browsers. It makes its money by taking a percentage of the value of any purchases made after users click on the sites it suggests.

If you download Invisible Hand and you then search for a satellite navigation system at a particular retailer, it will not only show you that product on your chosen retailer, it will also show you where that satellite navigation system is available at other retailers at a better price. It covers more than 100 retailers in three countries, including Best Buy, Amazon, Borders, Buy.com, The Home Depot, New Egg, Sears and Walmart. ▶

Products range from video games, toys, game consoles and consumer electronic devices to cosmetics, books and pharmaceuticals.

It is undeniably a great idea, but even great ideas need publicity to get the word out there. So in summer 2009 Invisible Hand hired Jargon PR to increase its number of downloads in the UK. Jargon is a PR agency based in Reading, with just five members of staff, and has been enthusiastically embracing online PR. 'Our clients used to view PR as just getting editorial coverage in traditional offline publications,' says Simon Corbett, Jargon's MD. 'They'd hire someone else to do all their online promotion. But increasingly that's changing. People are seeing the two as intrinsically linked and are bringing us on board to get them coverage and build them a buzz online and offline.'

Jargon began by finding around a dozen influential bloggers on the subject of Internet development and pointed them towards a free download of Invisible Hand. Once they had tried it out and had been impressed, they began discussing it in forums. Jargon contributed to and encouraged these conversations. Before long it was a hot subject in many forums. The third stage of the campaign was to go to online publications such as Lifehacker, Gizmodo and TechCrunch.

Corbett says: 'We didn't just do the traditional PR thing of enthusing about our great new service and expecting the writers to be excited by it. Instead we talked about how online purchasing is changing and how products like Invisible Hand are the future, and we offered the MD of the company as an expert commentator on this more general topic and gave real-world examples of savings that could be made.'

The tactic worked and many publications wrote about Invisible Hand. This meant that when Jargon PR finally approached offline titles, the team were able to point with confidence to the buzz that already existed around the product online. This encouraged those print journalists to write about it and so the buzz continued to grow.

It was remarkably successful. At the start of the campaign only a couple of thousand people had downloaded Invisible Hand; within a few weeks, and for a PR budget of just £8,000, this number had risen to more than 40,000. Corbett says: 'Campaigns like this show just what companies can achieve when they co-ordinate their PR work and look to manage their reputation across channels.'

brilliant recap

1 Marketers have long recognised the power of media editorial for shaping customers' opinions of their products and companies.

2 The Internet has changed the way marketers go about gaining that editorial coverage.

3 They are using online tools to contact journalists.

4 In recognition of the fact that a growing number of people read online publications and blogs, marketers are no longer focusing their PR efforts solely on traditional print media.

5 The best way to achieve positive editorial coverage – whether online or offline – is to target specific journalists with carefully considered and clearly expressed stories that are relevant to their readers.

6 By germinating a story amongst a small band of enthusiasts and then carefully spreading out to a more general readership, it is possible to create a campaign that has its own momentum.

CHAPTER 10

Mobile marketing

'The "Telephone" has too many shortcomings to be seriously considered as a means of communication.'

Western Union internal memo, 1876

What we'll cover in this chapter

With the widespread take-up of the smartphone, mobile marketing has finally become a reality. In this chapter you will find:

- the story of how online music retailer Zavvi.com used mobile marketing to generate £150,000 of revenue and add more than 10,000 new customers to its database in just one month;
- seven ways in which you can use mobile phones as a marketing tool;
- ten reasons why you should be interested in mobile marketing;
- advice on successful mobile marketing;
- an interview with Adhish Kulkarni, the MD of B!Digital UK, which claims to be the largest mobile-centric digital agency in the world.
- the story of how Birds Eye used mobile phones to run the most successful ever frozen food on-pack promotion in the UK.

2002 was going to be the year when mobile marketing really took off. So was 2003. And 2004, 2005, 2006, 2007, 2008 and 2009. By around 2007 most people had become understandably sceptical about these claims. The more credulous among us gave it until 2008 before concluding that it was nothing more than unjustified hype and mobile marketing was never really going to take off.

That might explain how so many marketers failed to notice that 2009 really was the year that mobile marketing took off. IAB and PwC research has revealed that in 2009 mobile ad spend grew by 32 per cent to £37.6 million. While still a drop in the ocean of overall ad spending, that represented rapid growth, especially when set against a significant decline in ad revenues in that year.

 **example**

Zavvi.com

Music retailer Zavvi folded on the high street in 2008 and relaunched online in November 2009 under new owners The Hut Group. As soon as it launched, Zavvi.com wanted to build a customer database and increase sales during the highly competitive Christmas period. It saw mobile as a key component in achieving this and so brought in mobile marketing agency Sponge.

The campaign was centred on a competition that was not only simple for consumers to enter but quick and cost-effective for Zavvi.com to set up. The plan was to help Zavvi.com generate a significant number of new customers in a short time at a low cost. Ads on billboards encouraged people to text in to be entered into a draw to win £1,000. All entrants received a unique code sent to their handsets to obtain a £1 discount on any order placed on the Zavvi.com website. The competition was promoted heavily on posters throughout the Tube network in London as well as on social media and deal forums. Over a one-month period in December 2009, 24,000 discount codes were issued. More than 19,000 were redeemed, generating more than £150,000 of revenue and adding more than 10,000 new customers to Zavvi.com's database.

'It's vital for retailers to consider m-commerce. It should be a key priority and they should be investing in the space,' said Richard Chapple, Commercial Director of The Hut Group. 'The way things are going, as handheld devices get smarter, more people will use them for things other than communication. I have an iPhone, and while it may not be the best handset in the world, I can do my grocery shopping on my way to an early morning meeting. It allows me to be more efficient with my time. There's a compelling opportunity for all businesses, especially retailers, to be using mobile as a trading tool.'

It was the launch of the iPhone that really made mobile marketing a possibility. It accelerated the development of the smartphone market, providing the necessary technology to millions of people and lowering the cost for those people to access the mobile web. As a result, mobile Internet usage increased by 21 per cent in 2009. By the end of the year 18.9 million handsets were accessing the mobile Internet every month, 77 per cent of mobile Internet sessions were exceeding five minutes and 23 per cent of all time spent accessing the Internet was on a mobile device.

Research carried out by Orange in 2010 revealed that more than half use their phones to access the Internet, 64 per cent send picture messages, 55 per cent play games, 49 per cent listen to music and 26 per cent receive email; 87 per cent use mobile media at home and 73 per cent when they are 'out and about'. Just under half said they used their phones to access the same sites they use on their PCs and 62 per cent said they wanted their phones to do the same things their PCs can.

Research firm Gartner has predicted that this trend will continue. It believes that by 2013 more than half of Internet users will be accessing the Web via mobiles and other handheld devices. In developing nations such as India, the majority of Internet activity already takes place on mobiles.

Over the next decade mobile bandwidth capacity is likely to increase between five- and ten-fold. That is going to create a major new space in which marketers will be able to reach their customers. So what are the ways in which marketers will be able to use that space?

Seven ways marketers can use mobile phones

1 SMS

Perhaps the most straightforward use of the mobile phone for marketing purposes is the promotional SMS, or text message. It can be a good way to deliver news, information or coupons which customers can redeem by taking their phones in-store or entering a code online.

It is a well-established channel but one that is becoming more and more popular. Recent research from Amplitude Research revealed that 73 per cent of people see texting as the most important feature they use on their phones.

2 Multimedia messages

For a higher impact but more expensive campaign, picture or video messages are a popular choice.

3 Bluetooth

Bluetooth is an alternative to WAP for broadcasting information. It is most popular amongst retail or leisure outlets which install the Bluetooth transmitter and then send out information to passers-by. It gives them a well-targeted opportunity to increase footfall with specific offers, promotions or product information.

4 Mobile games

Once it was Snake and Tetris; now mobile games are incredibly complex, sophisticated and popular. Marketers can take advantage in several ways: in game ads, pre-start ads or fully branded sponsorship.

 **example**

Sportswear manufacturer PUMA has a long association with motorsports, which it capitalised on with a 2008 mobile gaming campaign in China. To coincide with the Formula 1 race in Shanghai that year it created a mobile Internet site which included a PUMA F1 battle car-racing game. Successful players could win Ferrari shoes, bag and hat, and everyone who downloaded the game received directions to their nearest PUMA store and a coupon for a mobile phone toy accessory.

The game was downloaded 150,000 times, generating 185,000 new contacts for PUMA's marketing database and leading to 85 million page impressions on its website.

5 Mobile Internet

This is the major growth area. The rise of smartphones means that more than 20 per cent of all Internet access is from mobile phones and the experts believe this figure will continue to rise. This opens up a plethora of marketing opportunities.

According to the IAB/PwC report, in 2009 mobile search was the fastest growing format, up 41 per cent to £20.2 million. Mobile display, which includes banners and text links, grew by 24 per cent to £17.4 million.

> there has been much talk of augmented reality

In its January 2010 report on the mobile Internet industry, Gartner predicted that by 2013, more people will be accessing the web from mobile phones than from PCs. It believes that in 2013 there will be 1.78 billion PCs in use compared with 1.82 billion smartphones.

6 Applications

To date, more than 25,000 different applications have been made and downloaded 800 million times. It is a fast-growing market and one that allows marketers not only to advertise around apps created by other people but even to create their own apps that embed their brand deep within their customers' lives.

7 Location-based services

Most smartphones come with a global positioning satellite (GPS) receiver embedded and marketers are discovering the potential this offers. For example, there has been much talk of augmented reality, where users look through the camera view on their phones and see information superimposed on what they see. The information could be the time of the next train from the station they are looking at, or the lunch special in the restaurant across the road, or a special offer available in the shop they're passing.

Ten reasons why you should be interested in mobile marketing

1 Reach

According to comScore, in February 2009 there were 48 million people using mobile phones. The recent surge in the popularity of smartphones means that 15 million people interact with mobile media, disproving the theory that only teenagers and male gadget-geeks use mobile media. 42 per cent of users are female and the median age is 32.3. That is a reach and a demographic that few marketers can afford to ignore.

2 Cost

Compared with the cost of producing, printing and delivering direct mail, mobile marketing is inexpensive. For example, at the time of writing, a straightforward SMS marketing campaign cost around 4p per text sent.

3 One-to-one and ultra-responsive

A key feature of mobile marketing is that you deliver it to a specific number and so you know who will receive your message. This allows you to tailor your communications with a high degree of accuracy. Partly because of this personalisation, and partly because it is easy for people to respond to campaigns via a mobile phone, it is an especially responsive medium.

4 Always on

Research by Orange has found that of those who use mobile media, 81 per cent do so more than once a week and 47 per cent use it every day. We speed past billboards, we turn off our tele-visions and we close our Internet browsers, but our mobile phones are pretty much always on.

5 Build your own media channel through apps

The explosion of interest in smartphone applications offers marketers a major branding opportunity. Develop your own content or sponsor someone else's – however you do it, you can associate your brand with information or entertainment that really engages your customers.

6 Direct revenue opportunities

On top of this branding potential apps offer a way to directly generate revenue. According to analysts Frost & Sullivan, in 2009 there were 2.7 billion app downloads from the iPhone alone. Around 20.5 per cent were paid-for downloads, at an average price of $3.55. The total app revenue from this one brand of smartphone alone was $1.96 billion. Frost & Sullivan estimates that by 2014 this will rise to $8.2 billion.

7 Data capture

Mobile campaigns are well placed to capture data about users. It is quick and easy for users to key in and send information on their location, gender, age, job and so on. It is also easy to link mobile campaigns to on-pack purchases and so build up data about an individual's purchasing habits.

8 Portability

The mobile phone is the very definition of the portable device. This not only increases the amount of time available for you to contact your customers, it also allows you to link your campaigns to specific locations. For example, you can drive footfall to a shop, restaurant, gallery and so on by having a Bluetooth message or SMS sent to people within a certain radius. To give another example, you can use the GPS function on smartphones to direct users to nearby branches of retailers, banks, etc.

9 Complements other marketing channels

Mobile campaigns integrate well into other marketing channels. In fact, many marketers use it as a quick, easy-access point to the broader campaign. So consumers will send a text message, or click on a mobile ad, to receive a direct mail pack or a telemarketing call.

10 Good place to innovate

People have expectations of what they want to see in traditional offline advertising. Increasingly, they have such expectations with much online marketing. There is now a rigid way to structure a marketing e-mail. Mobile, however, is a newer space and so recipients are much less hidebound by conventions. Mobile media users aren't scared of seeing new things on their phones. In fact, according to Orange's research, 70 per cent of mobile media users find new and innovative advertising formats appealing. This means there is more room for you to innovate and to try out new ideas that you can then apply elsewhere in your marketing mix.

How to do it successfully

1 Don't assume it's a channel populated solely by young men

As the figures above show, a wide range of people use mobile media, so always begin any campaign by discovering who uses mobile in your audience and in what way. Which aspect of mobile do they use? When and where? How? What do they want from it?

2 Delivery is cheap, so invest in good quality creative

One of the great mistakes with mobile marketing – as with all digital marketing – is assuming that because delivery mechanisms are relatively inexpensive, this can be treated as marketing on the cheap. The result is almost always a campaign that looks cheap, fails and thus turns out to be a waste of money. Instead, invest in your creative. Make sure you develop engaging mobile campaign experiences for all users, regardless of the handset they use.

3 Ensure your response mechanism works

You also need to spend money on your response mechanism. It is no good having the most compelling SMS campaign or app if it directs people to a .mobi site that they can't see or that looks very different to the initial contact.

At the same time, ensure you encourage response. Mobile phones naturally lend themselves to response, but you can make it easier or more appealing for consumers to do so. Give them something for their time, such as a free download, a chance to win something or a coupon offering a discount.

4 Think about frequency of contact

Don't blanket message customers if they have trusted you by giving you their details. Think carefully about the experiences that will be most relevant to them. Start with what you think your customers would like, not what you'd like to sell them.

Ideally you should run an opt-in-only campaign. This is the surest way to encourage engagement with your campaign and to preserve mobile as an effective marketing channel. At the very least, you should offer your mobile contacts a way of opting out of receiving messages, such as sending the word 'stop'.

5 Don't see mobile purely as a cost

mobile applications present opportunities for branding and revenue generation

Few marketers are attuned to think about how to make money directly from their campaigns. They see them as a way to generate sales leads. Mobile applications present opportunities for branding and revenue generation, so shift your mindset.

6 Use data

Far too many marketers faithfully collect data on their customers and those who respond to their campaigns, but then fail to use it. They store it away in expensive customer relationship management (CRM) systems where it gathers dust and decays. Make good use of your data, enhancing it with some of the growing datasets – such as lifestyle or behavioural data – that are becoming more widely available and more accurately populated. Use this information to produce campaigns that are more relevant to your prospects.

7 Stop thinking about your message

One of the reasons an application is successful is that it *does*, rather than says, something. This can be quite a shift in thinking for traditional marketers. Create experiences and tools people will find useful.

8 Remember that mobile phones are ... mobile

More and more mobile phones incorporate GPS technology which gives you an absolutely vital piece of information about your prospects: where they are. Think about how you can use location in your campaigns to deliver the right message, at the right time and in the right place.

9 Integrate with other channels

Ensure you maintain a consistent brand and message across all your channels and think about how your mobile campaigns can reinforce your other digital and even your offline campaigns.

10 Innovate!

Above all else, mobile marketing is a place to be brave, to try out the great ideas you have waiting in the wings but have always been too afraid to try out. Mobile media users expect to see something a little different, so give it a go and see what happens.

Expert interview: Adhish Kulkarni, Managing Director, B!Digital UK

B!Digital UK claims to be the largest mobile-centric digital agency in the world. From its offices in the UK, France, Spain, Germany, Italy, Russia, the Netherlands and the USA, B!Digital builds campaigns for brands such as Orange Wednesdays, O2 Top Up Surprises, HP, Sky Remote Record and Vodafone Egypt. Adhish Kulkarni has worked in this industry for seven years, having previously worked at Flytxt, one of the original mobile marketing innovators. He moved to B!Digital when Flytxt was acquired by the Buongiorno group – the current owners – in 2007.

AB: Why should readers be interested in mobile marketing?

AK: Mobile is the future. It's an important channel that no digital marketer can ignore. With more than 4 billion mobile phones in the world, mobile advertising is expected to grow exponentially. Abi Research has predicted that it will reach $29 billion by 2014.

AB: Sure, mobile phones are popular, but what are the specific benefits of mobile marketing?

AK: Mobile is personal and ubiquitous, interactive, transactional and viral.

AB: I can see how it could be on smartphones that allow Web access. But few of those 4 billion old phones are smartphones.

AK: True, but usage is increasing exponentially. In 2009, in Japan, the percentage of web pages visited from mobile devices compared with those visited from a PC reached 65 per cent, and it is forecast that by 2012 the most sold Internet device will be a smartphone.

AB: But why do we need to look at this as a different topic from online marketing? Aren't smartphones just a new way to access and view the Internet?

AK: Mobile is not just an extension of the Internet, it is a platform in its own right. The mobile Web will be bigger than most people seem to think. In fact, according to Morgan Stanley, the Internet itself is being driven to a new stage by two concurrent phenomena: social networking and mobile.

AB: How can marketers use mobile phones as a marketing channel?

AK: You can sell content, capture data, broadcast information, interact with customers and deliver advertising. All this has emerged in just the ten years since the start of mobile marketing. There is much still to come.

AB: How can a marketer get started with mobile marketing?

AK: First, they should empower a small team comprising legal, operations, marketing and IT to garner support from the key stakeholders in the organisation. This is an essential first step as it lays the foundations for rapid decision making.

AB: What next?

AK: For any marketer embarking on a mobile marketing campaign, it is critical to answer a series of questions about their customers in order to ensure mobile is a suitable channel and that they use it to best effect.

AB: What are those questions?

AK: What kind of phones do they carry? How phone-savvy are they? How do you speak to the customer today? How often? What tone? This is critical to address in order to select the optimal mix of mobile channels and frequency of messages to the audience. For example, while it may be fine for a drinks brand to speak to customers every week, it's probably better for an insurance company to interact once a quarter.

AB: That raises an important point. Don't people see their phones as quite personal to them? How do they react to companies sending them marketing messages on their phones?

AK: It's essential to build trust in the relationship. Mobile is personal and so when entering into a conversation with a customer the company needs to be transparent – there must be an explicit opt-in – and relevant. Do both of those things and your customers will welcome your mobile contact.

AB: Have you got an example of someone who's done that well?

AK: Absolutely. Smash Hits, the now defunct magazine, used to message its user base once a week, but always with relevant teen gossip. Opt-out rates were almost zero.

AB: What about applications? Is there potential for them to be used by marketers?

AK: Huge potential. But again it is vital to be relevant and useful. The most successful apps are the ones that are useful to the customers. Whether it is entertaining, informing or simply improving the customer's life, a mobile promotion should be relevant and useful to the customer to ensure repeat usage and increase brand equity.

AB: Have you got an example of someone that's achieved that with apps?

AK: A great one was a paint company in the US which released a mobile app which took a colour that the user had photographed and matched it to the closest paint product.

AB: What about integration with other channels?

AK: Mobile can be a standalone channel, but it works best when leveraging other media. There is no point in creating a campaign and then adding mobile as an afterthought. It probably won't work and even if it does, it is never as effective as integrating the advantages of mobile into the campaign from the outset.

AB: How can it be integrated?

AK: A code on a poster can make it interactive, a shortcode on-pack can enable an instant win. An advertisement can teach people how to download an app and an online sign-up can deliver coupons when you are in store to your handset. Ensure as a marketer that all the available channels are being leveraged to promote mobile and vice versa.

AB: Again, do you have a good example of this integration?

AK: Orange Wednesdays is a great example of this. It uses above-the-line advertising and below-the-line marketing to pull customers into the programme, after which the relationship between brand and customer continues on WAP, Web and SMS.

AB: Tell me more about Orange Wednesdays.

AK: Orange Wednesdays is the world's largest mobile vouchering campaign outside Japan. Each week in the UK, Orange customers can request a mobile voucher via SMS, WAP or by dialling 241. This voucher allows them to take a friend to watch any film for free on Wednesdays at any cinema in the country. We manage the delivery of the vouchers direct to the handsets and manage a wireless redemption terminal network in cinemas across the country. The promotion was recently extended to include a 2-4-1 offer at Pizza Express on Wednesdays.

The plan is to associate the Orange brand with rewards that could not easily be replicated by any competitor. By delivering it through the mobile phone, Orange has not only made it easy for its customers to access the promotion, it has also allowed the company to capture data on those customers and so personalise messages.

By November 2009 Orange had delivered 20 million vouchers, of which 55 per cent had been redeemed. It receives an average of 500,000 voucher requests every month.

AB: That's a great example. Do you have any others?

AK: There's HP in the US, which uses us to enable a product review service that provides instant advice via WAP on products in store, so customers can get help on which product to buy even when there is no one in store available to help.

AB: What's new, interesting and cutting edge in this area right now?

AK: Integrating one of the key capabilities of smartphones – location – into campaigns allows for a highly targeted and therefore more successful approach.

AB: Anything else?

AK: Mobile couponing is also shaping up to be a key trend. As technology improves and allows for more sophisticated methods of redemption, both by the retailer and via the actual handset, retailers are beginning to see the value of mobile couponing, especially when combined with location capabilities for driving footfall.

 example

Birds Eye

Birds Eye needs little introduction. More than eight in every ten households buy Birds Eye products and the company is part of the Birds Eye Iglo Group, the market-leading frozen foods business in Europe.

When Birds Eye approached its marketing agency, The Big Kick, to develop an on-pack campaign, it specified several objectives: increase sales, encourage purchase of multiple products, develop loyalty and win back lapsed customers. The Big Kick brought mobile specialist Sponge on board to help it achieve those ambitious goals.

The team immediately recognised that mobile is an ideal way to communicate with busy mums on the go who are looking to prepare a quick and nutritional meal for their children. The key was to devise a promotional mechanism that would be quick enough that those mums would have the time to do it and high enough value that they would want to do so.

The campaign was primarily aimed at 'Striving Mums', aged under 44, C2D with children, making up 13.1 per cent of the population. Secondary target audiences were 'Safety Seekers', aged 45–64, C1DE, making up 12.9 per cent of the population, and 'Great British Cooks', aged over 65, E, making up 20.2 per cent of the population. Birds Eye wanted to gain a deeper understanding of its customer base in these areas and to capture information on their purchase preferences.

The campaign centred on an eye-catching prize: 'Be Mortgage Free'. There were two tiers of prizes to be won: £1,000 daily over 106 days, with all entrants entered into a second draw for a monthly prize for one winner who would have their mortgage paid off. The promotion ran for three months, so there would be three lucky winners.

The choice of mortgage was highly emotive. For most people their home is more than just a roof over their heads; it represents the opportunity for financial freedom. It was decided to use insurance for the top prize to ensure that there was no maximum limit to the value of the mortgage reimbursed, irrespective of whether the consumer lived in a studio or a stately home. Furthermore, if the winner did not have a mortgage they could choose a cash alternative of £100,000 or they could pass the prize on to their offspring.

The promotion featured on 50 million units of Birds Eye products, across 42 product ranges from Fish Fingers to Garden Peas. In order to make it quick and easy for those busy mums to enter, the primary entry method was to text in a unique code that was found in each product pack to a shortcode, although consumers were also able to enter via the Web and by post.

On behalf of Birds Eye, Sponge contacted entrants three times: immediately on entry, 24 hours later with the results of the previous day's £1,000 draw, and at the beginning of the following month with the results of the monthly mortgage draw. As well as responding to the consumer on these three occasions with the factual information relating to their entry, Sponge also used dynamic messaging to include a personal targeted message to the entrants, based on the purchases they had made to enter the competition. These messages were selected from three different databases. There was nutritional advice, such as 'Peas contain more fibre than the same amount of Baked Beans' or 'Did you know five Birds Eye Chicken Dippers have less saturated fat than one Pork sausage?'. There were recipe ideas, such as 'Have you tried making a Birds Eye Fish Finger Pie? Layer fish fingers, beans and mash!'. This was useful to mums, 70 per cent of whom at 4pm every day don't know what they will feed their family that evening. Finally, there were cross-sell messages. These were designed to fulfil Birds Eye's goal of encouraging its consumers to buy across categories. Messages included 'Bored with chips? Try Birds Eye Potato Waffles' and 'If you like our Steam Fresh Vegetables you'll love our Garden Peas'.

This activity produced impressive results. The campaign generated 1.8 million entries, representing a 3.6 per cent response rate, making it the most successful frozen food on-pack promotion in the UK. Each consumer entered on average 2.1 times and more than 100,000 consumers opted in to receive ongoing product and recipe information via email.

Furthermore, more than 5 per cent of participants 'made and played' – they followed the purchase recommendation and then entered a second time with the code from their new purchase. This ensured the campaign met the initial objectives of not only increasing sales but also encouraging purchase of multiple products and developing loyalty.

 recap

1 After many years of inflated expectations it seems as though mobile marketing has finally arrived.

2 This has been prompted by the rapid growth since 2008 of smartphone usage. It is predicted that this will accelerate in the future and that mobile marketing will grow in importance.

3 At its simplest, mobile marketing is SMS-based. Beyond this there is a spectrum of complexity, from video messages to mobile Internet, apps and games, all the way through to location-based marketing.

4 Get it right and mobile marketing can provide an unrivalled combination of reach, responsiveness, user engagement, data collection and portability.

5 The best mobile marketing campaigns are quick and easy for consumers to enter when out and about.

CONCLUSION

A marketing revolution

'The trouble with the future it that it usually arrives before we're ready for it.'

Arnold H. Glasgow

The Internet is really changing marketing. In this book we have looked at the techniques that are emerging. From website design through search, online advertising, e-mail marketing and so on, they are presenting a vast new array of opportunities to get in front of consumers and deliver marketing messages.

However, marketing is changing more fundamentally than that. The Internet has done more than just provide a few new channels. It is radically altering the way in which marketers communicate with their audiences. It is early days yet, but we are witnessing a revolution in the world of marketing; the marketers who get to grips with it now are the ones who will flourish in the months and years ahead.

Throughout this book you will have noticed that alongside the different techniques covered in each chapter there are a number of themes that crop up. These are the principles that those marketers – you – need to grasp if they are to succeed in the world of online marketing. Here they are in summary.

1 You're not in control any more

Traditionally, marketing has been based on two assumptions: that companies were the main sources of information about their products and services and that you could attract potential customers through advertising, direct marketing and so on. Both assumptions have been irreversibly undermined by the Internet.

No one listens to people who broadcast marketing messages. Try to push your message on to people and they will rapidly back away. They are wise to what you're doing and they have plenty of other sources of information. The new marketing is about engaging with consumers in their spaces and giving them content that will draw them to you.

2 Investment in quality online content is rarely wasted

Once you have accepted that we are playing a radically different game from the one we played just a decade ago, you need to get to work on developing content that will pull potential customers towards you.

This could be information on how to use your products or it could be discount codes, event invitations or special offers. Whatever it is, and whichever medium you use to convey it, it needs to be genuinely compelling to your prospects. The focus needs to be on the customer, not on the product. The old approach of simply talking up your company and products will no longer work.

Spend time on that content and be prepared to bring in the experts to help you create it. Above all else, remember the importance of brands. No one is attracted to dull, faceless organisations; people want to know who you are and what you believe in. So be brave. Take a position and stick with it. Build a brand. People will be drawn to you.

3 You must continually innovate on distribution techniques

How you package your content matters and it changes continually. Do not limit yourself to text. Make good use of rich media such as podcasts, WebTV and mobile media. Whatever format you choose to distribute your messages, ensure that they are search engine friendly. Be constantly on the lookout for new techniques.

4 You need to promote through social media and search

While it is true to some extent that if you build it they will come, you need to start the ball rolling. The trick is to use online promotional techniques to subtly seed your new content. Social media is ideal for this. It allows you to drop your new campaign naturally into conversations with existing contacts. If it is sufficiently exciting then they will tell their contacts and so on until people you have never heard of are searching for you. Because your site and your content are properly optimised, those strangers need only tap your brand name into a search engine and they have found you in two clicks of the mouse.

5 Online marketing should not stand alone

All these online marketing techniques can be immensely powerful on their own, but as we have seen, they are most effective when used in combination, and in the same way they are even more effective when used in conjunction with traditional offline techniques. After all, people are still more likely to click on the link of a brand they have heard of.

Finally, then, bear in mind that online marketing is no quick fix. It takes time. In the early days a handful of people had sudden, enormous success and this has fooled many people into believing that that is what online marketing is all about. I hope that this book has shown that this is not the case.

Online marketing has grown up. It is now less about taking a chance on some edgy innovation that could take your brand global; it is more about consistently applying sophisticated and complex techniques over a sustained period. It may be less exciting, but it is more reliable. And as we have also seen in this book, it is possible to define processes to make online marketing work for you, to make it generate leads, increase sales and raise profits. For the serious marketer, that is what is truly exciting.

GLOSSARY

One of the main barriers to successful online marketing is the baffling array of jargon and acronyms employed by those who work in the industry. Very often it seems that as soon as the general business world has caught up with the meaning of one acronym or buzzword, the online marketing industry invents a new one just to keep us on our toes. Throughout this book I have tried to avoid the more meaningless techspeak and to explain words that may be unfamiliar to the typical reader. Here is a glossary of some of the terms and acronyms that may be unfamiliar but which have not been explained in the book.

Algorithm A set of rules for solving a problem in a finite number of steps; search engines use them to rank websites depending on what the user has searched for.

Applications (apps) Programs that users can download to their mobile phones.

Banner ad An ad that sits along the top of the web page.

Biometric data Information used to identify individuals; most typically this is fingerprints or retina scans.

Bouncebacks E-mails that are returned undelivered to the sender.

Brochure site A straightforward website that simply provides information about the company in question.

CPA (cost per action) You pay a set amount for every action, such as a sale or an enquiry, that results from a user clicking your ad. Types of CPA are cost per lead (CPL) and cost per sale (CPS).

CPC (cost per click) You pay a set amount each time someone clicks on your ad.

CPD (cost per day) Close to a traditional payment model for advertising, you pay for each day your ad is live on the site.

CPM (cost per mille) You pay for every 1,000 impressions of your ad. An impression is a site serving the page containing your ad to a visitor, so in essence CPM is you paying a set amount for 1,000 people to view your ad.

De-duping technology Software that scans your database, identifying and eliminating duplicate entries.

Domain name A series of letters and numbers used to name organisations and computers and addresses on the Internet.

E-commerce Buying and selling online.

Galvanic Producing or caused by an electric current.

Hypertext Markup Language (HTML) The standard protocol for formatting and displaying documents on the World Wide Web.

Internet Advertising Bureau (IAB) Trade association for those involved in online advertising.

Internet Advertising Sales Houses (IASH) Group formed to encourage best practice among online advertising sales houses through the adoption of an effective code of conduct.

Internet service provider (ISP) A company that provides access to the Internet.

Landing page Web page where users arrive after clicking on a certain link.

Microsite A small site which is usually connected to your main one, but which contains specific information on a particular product, service or campaign.

Multivariant tests Tests which allow you to test many different variables at the same time.

Overlay ad An ad that covers – or overlays – the page the user is viewing.

Personal digital assistant (PDA) A handheld computer.

Podcast A web-based audio broadcast.

Rich media Any content that is more complex than simple text.

Site architecture The structure of a website.

Tracking cookie A small piece of data left on your computer to indicate that you have visited a particular website.

User-initiated rich media ad Usually an ad that runs before a video clip that the user has downloaded.

Video blog A blog delivered via a video.

Web 2.0 A term commonly used to describe the phase of the Internet when it shifted from being about information to being about communication; usually closely associated with the emergence of social media.

Webcast An online broadcast.

Widget A piece of code that a website owner can simply take and use to add a particular function to that site.

Wireframe A basic visual guide to a website's structure.

Index